ASBOA

THE END OF MEMBERSHIP
AS WE KNOW IT

*Building the Fortune-Flipping, Must-Have
Association of the Next Century*

SARAH L. SLADEK

The Center for Association Leadership

WASHINGTON, DC

ASAE: The Center for Association Leadership
1575 I Street, NW
Washington, DC 20005-1103
Phone: (202) 626-2723; (888) 950-2723 outside the metropolitan Washington, DC area
Fax: (202) 220-6439
Email: books@asaecenter.org
We connect great ideas and great people to inspire leadership and achievement in the association community.

Keith C. Skillman, CAE, Vice President, Publications, ASAE: The Center for Association Leadership
Baron Williams, CAE, Director of Book Publishing, ASAE: The Center for Association Leadership

Cover and interior by Troy Scott Parker, Cimarron Design

This book is available at a special discount when ordered in bulk quantities. For information, contact the ASAE Member Service Center at (202) 371-0940.

A complete catalog of titles is available on the ASAE website at www.asaecenter.org.

ISBN-13: 978-0-88034-343-5
ISBN-10: 0-88034-343-5

Printed in the United States of America.

10 9 8 7 6 5 4 3 2 1

To my bright and beautiful daughters who, by their very existence, make me want to make the world a better place. Every day is an adventure, every dream a possibility.

And to my mentor, Jeff Leitner, for keeping me focused on shooting hoops instead of hitting fly balls. You are annoyingly right about everything and you challenge me more than anyone else and I'm grateful for that.

Contents

1

The Making of a
Dominant Association

"Prosperity tries the fortunate;
adversity the great."
Rose F. Kennedy

After a boom on the stock market that enticed many everyday
people to invest their entire savings, the stock market crashed on
October 29, 1929. The crash marked the beginning of a decade
of high unemployment, poverty, low profits, deflation, plunging
farm incomes, and lost opportunities for economic growth and
personal advancement. Although its causes are still uncertain
and controversial, the net effect was a sudden and general loss
of confidence in the economic future. America's economy was at
an all-time low, slumping into the Great Depression, followed by
World War II.

Times were tough, but recovery soon followed. In 1946, the
war was over, the economy was thriving, and the first Baby
Boomers were born. Their parents would encourage them
to attend college, work hard, raise families, and pursue the
American Dream. This generation would be raised to give
generously of their time and money to community organizations and causes. The Baby Boomer generation would become

passionate about joining, volunteering, and serving membership associations.

While membership associations have been in existence since the 1600s, we can look back in history and see that the time between 1946 and 2000 were stand-out years for most associations. The active support of the Boomers, the largest generation in American history, coupled with the participation of their predecessors, the Traditional Generation, membership associations thrived. We can even go so far as to say that membership associations dominated both the professional and personal social structures.

In economics, a monopoly exists when an enterprise has sufficient control over a particular product or service to determine the terms under which other individuals shall have access to it. Monopolies survive when there is a lack of economic competition. For years, membership associations were in many ways like monopolies, dominant in our culture; they offered a valuable commodity, members paid dues to have access to the commodity, and competition was minimal.

From 1995 to 2000, stock markets in industrialized nations saw their equity value rise rapidly from growth in the evolving internet sector. The period was marked by the founding of a group of new internet-based companies commonly referred to as "dot-coms." A combination of rapidly increasing stock prices, market confidence that the companies would turn future profits, individual speculation in stocks, and widely available venture capital created an environment in which many investors were willing to overlook traditional metrics in favor of confidence in technological advancements.

Yet, as the saying goes, what goes up must come down. Starting in 2000, associations would experience a barrage of challenges that would weaken their positions in the marketplace and forever alter their futures. Eventually, the bubble burst. In just six days—from March 10 to March 15, 2000—the NASDAQ lost nearly nine percent. Hiring freezes, layoffs, and consolidations followed in several industries.

On September 11, 2001, terrorists attacked New York and Washington DC, intentionally crashing two airplanes into the World Trade Center and another into the Pentagon. A fourth plane crashed into a field after the crew and passengers tried to retake control of the plane. In the aftermath of this tragic day, many associations suffered substantial losses in meeting and event attendance and were forced to not only consider new options for delivering content and value to members but also become a resource to help their members through these tragic times.

On October 6, 2008, the Great Recession began. The stock market spiraled into a week-long decline in which the Dow Jones Industrial Average fell 18.1 percent. The financial crisis was triggered by a liquidity shortfall in the United States banking system and resulted in the collapse of large financial institutions, the bailout of banks by national governments, and downturns in stock markets around the world.

For the United States in particular, persistent unemployment, the continuing decline in home values, an escalating federal debt crisis, inflation, and rising gas prices continue to plague the country at the time this book is being written in 2011.

On January 1, 2011, America's organizations braced themselves for the retirement wave. For years our nation's leaders have been concerned about the arrival of 2011. It's long been predicted that this will be the year that launches our nation's enterprises into a downward spiral composed of retirement waves and talent turnover. Some have even referred to it as "the perfect storm" that will leave organizations at risk of losing critical knowledge and unable to fill valuable positions vacated by the Boomers.

The Great Recession may have softened the blow that was once expected, as some Boomers opt to postpone their retirements. Nonetheless, this year alone, 2.8 million Americans will turn 65. Between now and 2030, 78 million Boomers will retire, which marks the beginning of the end of the workforce as we have known it.

Looking Forward

Will this decade of economic catastrophe lead to decades of prosperity? Perhaps we're on the brink of another economic boom, and just as America once evolved from a country plagued with economic depression and war in the 1930s and 1940s, America will prosper again. Perhaps not.

We can't predict the future with any certainty, but we do know that associations have forever been altered. What associations are facing today is significantly more substantial than what associations faced in the 1930s and 1940s. Recovering from war and financial decline was certainly a struggle. But in addition to recovering from recent tragedies, the United States today is also being forced to manage unprecedented change—the kind of change that will substantially affect the way we work, live, and do business.

Since the 1600s, the inner workings and overall purposes of membership associations had remained the same. Two key factors have evolved that will prevent associations from ever having success by doing things the way they have been done for the past three centuries: technology and demographic shifts.

Rapid advances in technology have changed—and continue to change—the way we communicate with one another. More technology has been developed in the past five years than the previous 50 years.

The speed and breadth of technology is unprecedented and often overwhelming, as our society is being challenged to continually adapt to and integrate new technological advancements. Furthermore, entire generations that have never known life without technology are now entering the workforce.

Technology has been a game-changer, giving people access to networks and information without the assistance of associations. Yet, the hurdle that technology poses pales in comparison to the generational shift that's about to occur in the 21st century.

From now until 2030, every eight seconds someone will turn 65. This shift in human capital—the largest shift in our country's history—poses the greatest threat to associations because most associations remain entirely governed and supported by the Baby Boomer generation, and few have or are developing strategies to cushion themselves from this massive exodus of board members, committee chairs, and dedicated volunteers. According to BoardSource's Nonprofit Governance Index, only 2 percent of board members are under 30 years old.

Coupled with social changes that have emerged in the last 20 years, such as work-life balance and a societal movement away from conformity towards individuality, we now have generations with dramatically different needs, values, wants, and expectations.

Like it or not, joining an association doesn't necessarily top the next generation's list of things to do.

On the heels of the recent recession, members of all ages are likely questioning the value of membership in your association, but the youngest will continue to pose this question for the next 19 years. They demand a return on investment unlike any other generation that has come before them. *Generations and the*

Future of Association Participation, published by The William E. Smith Institute for Association Research (2006), noted that younger people seek and demand a return for membership, including tangible member services, high levels of accountability, identifiable career advantages, a sense of professional community, and opportunities to serve within associations.

Borrowing an excerpt from my book, *The New Recruit: What Your Association Needs to Know About X, Y, & Z* (2007):

> "The Boomer-centric associations still think they can launch something new and it will resolve all their recruiting woes. These associations have overlooked the simple fact that the vast majority of their membership will retire in the next decade or two—and the generations to follow are radically different from the generations of the past two centuries.
>
> Membership associations have not experienced anything like this before. Generations X and Y have completely different values, interests, needs, and wants from the generations before them. Their worldview, their priorities—everything about them is different as a result of their social experiences.
>
> Generations X and Y will not respond to the recruiting efforts of the past. An entirely new approach is required. Everything about the membership association has to change....
>
> The Boomer-centric associations will refuse to change or fear change. These are the associations that are considered endangered species and likely will be extinct by the year 2020. The New Recruit associations realize the need to recruit and retain younger members and invites younger generations in to help them make the change. These are the associations that will succeed and survive."

The dominance that associations once celebrated is now crumbling. Membership has lost its meaning amid an audience that no longer wants or needs to be members, partly because of technology and partly because of differing values shared by young generations. In other words, technology and demographic shifts are rendering associations irrelevant. As we examine where associations have been and what the future is likely to bring, it begs the question: Is survival possible?

The answer is a resounding "yes"! Associations can rebuild their dominance and be successful in the years to come if they can accept that the rules have changed. What worked in the past isn't going to work anymore.

The economy will eventually recover, but that doesn't mean going back to business as usual. Technology is here to stay and the demographic shift is just beginning. Now, more than ever, associations need to be able to prove beyond a doubt that membership provides a return on investment to their members—especially its youngest members and prospects. Even the concept of the transactional membership—paying dues for access to member benefits—is under question. This book explores in greater detail new membership models and definitions of membership. You will find that some associations have moved away from paid membership altogether.

But before we delve too far into the details of changing membership models, there are three components to consider when rebuilding your association. Without these elements in place, it will be virtually impossible to recruit and retain members or generate substantial profits.

Association Must-Haves

The goal is to build your association into a dominant, membership-attracting, revenue-generating organization, to stand out from all others as the single best association in your industry. As in business, your association will become dominant in the market if, and only if, what you provide is incredibly valuable and the competition is minimal.

The following elements (or a lack of them) will determine whether your association is capable of making a return to dominance.

Niche

A few years ago, I was hired by a trade association that was struggling to grow membership. At my first meeting with the association executives, I posed the question about target market. Who were their current and prospective members? I jotted down their answers, which ended up being a list of 10 different markets, representing a variety of industries in a variety of locations. When I asked them to narrow their answer down to one audience, they couldn't do it.

I find this in my work with chambers of commerce as well. One chamber I was working with hadn't seen an upswing in membership for seven years. When I asked the chamber president about target market, he told me the chamber's target market was any and all businesses operating in a 75-mile radius of the city.

In both these situations, the prospective market for these organizations was gigantic! One would think they'd be capable of drawing in hundreds of new members every month, and yet they both struggled to recruit even a dozen, and retention was also on the decline. Why? Because trying to be all things to all people is a sure way to fail. Niches are what all successful products and services have in common, without exception. There is money in niches!

The association of yesteryear focused on quantity—getting as many members as possible without alienating anyone. When you take this route, you will find more competition; your approach will be generalized; your information will be watered-down; and you will be doing twice as much work just to keep up.

In a world with more access to information and more competition than ever before, your association needs to be the go-to resource for one audience. You need to set yourself apart as the "expert," providing ample resources in your area of expertise, thereby making it easy for those who need you to find you and to find value in joining your association.

This isn't a one-size-fits-all world anymore. Seek to be meaningful to someone—not everyone—and the rest will follow.

Culture

Throughout my career, I've had the opportunity to interact with associations nationwide. I can tell you with absolute certainty that culture makes a significant difference in how effective your association is at recruiting and retaining members and generating revenue. I have observed associations with positive, engaging, service-oriented cultures and those with cultures that are inclusive, close-minded, and downright off-putting. I've even observed associations with hostile cultures. Most of the time, associations with a negative culture don't even realize they have such a culture, or if they do realize it, they struggle to correct it.

Here are a few red flags that will pop up when culture is a concern: high turnover among staff, volunteers, or board; difficulty recruiting or retaining members; negative feedback from your members or others; emotional outbursts (e.g., arguments, storming out of meetings); or no-shows (e.g., board members' not showing up for meetings or continually calling in excuses for not being able to attend the meetings).

Culture is not something you can actually see, yet it is in the environment and experiences your association creates for its members. In many ways, culture is like personality. It's the values, beliefs, underlying assumptions, experiences, and habits that create your association's behavior and ways of working together. Culture is especially influenced by the organization's founder, executives, and other managerial staff because of their roles in decision making and strategic direction. Your association's website, the interaction of board members in meetings, and the way in which people collaborate when they volunteer speak volumes about your organizational culture.

Here's why culture matters: Younger generations are driven by personal happiness. They refuse to engage in anything negative, challenging, or draining of their time and energy. They will also refuse to engage in a culture that isn't open to them. Your association could have a great culture as it relates to customer service but fall short on technology or engaging young people as board members and committee leaders.

If you suspect your culture has taken a turn for the worse, it may be time for a change in leadership, some customer service or team-building training, a marketing audit, member surveys, staff retreats, coaching—anything that may help your organization pinpoint the source of negativity, effectively resolve conflict, or improve member relations.

Boomers are driven by the opportunity to serve and will gladly make an effort to "fix" whatever is ailing your association. That's not the case with Generations X and Y. They expect a great experience and want to affiliate themselves with a great cause. Negative, unorganized, stressful situations are a sure-fire way to create an escape hatch for them.

Bottom line: You must eliminate the negative and accentuate the positive to engage your next-generation membership.

Dues

Some people would rather get a root canal than delve into the topic of dues. I don't blame them. When you're talking about separating people from their money, the discussion can get emotional. Nevertheless, we're coming off the worst recession in seven decades, and in the coming years your association will have to answer less to people who willingly pay dues "because it's the right thing to do" and more to people who continually ask, "What's in this for me?" This means your association continually will have to prove its worth, whether you are charging $5 or $5,000 for a membership.

How do you prove the value of a membership in your association? Actually, this question is less about number-crunching and more about marketing. Here's how to break it down:

→ For starters, what does your association do?

As simple as this may sound, the way you choose to answer this very question is the difference between your prospects' eyes glazing over and reaching for their checkbooks.

Younger generations are your toughest consumers, and they want to associate themselves with a cause. They want to be inspired to make a difference. So does your association represent independent gas companies (yawn) or is it helping bring cheaper gas to the United States quicker (wow!)? Does your chamber of commerce connect businesses (yawn) or does it bring in an average of $25,000 in new business to members each year (wow!)?

See the difference?

And as long as we're on the topic, it's worth pointing out a few things your association shouldn't do. Never, ever make a habit of resting on your laurels or cite networking as a member benefit. Too many associations make the mistake of launching every conversation, speech, and website paragraph with some verbiage about how long they've been in existence. The fact that your association has been around 100 years may be an interesting, even impressive, factoid, but this shouldn't be the primary focus of all your messaging. It is not what you do and it has nothing to do with where you are going, which is really what your members want to know.

Likewise, when I ask association executives what a key benefit is for joining their association, 99 percent of them say "networking." Networking is not a member benefit! It's an activity that may result from joining an association, but it's certainly not exclusive to your association, so it shouldn't be your association's primary claim to fame. Thanks to technology, people can easily find the people they want to network with and they don't need your association to do it.

When you talk about your association and what it does, it shouldn't sound like a textbook or instruction manual or a bill on Capitol Hill (yawn!). Make sure it's meaningful, unique, and motivates people to take action. Grab your audience, get them to sit up and say "wow!" and they will gladly join you.

→ Next, how does your association add value to the lives of your members?

This takes the what-you-do conversation a step farther. Rather than just coming up with elaborate content that is authored by professionals, you are taking key information right from your members themselves. You can capture this information from surveys or interviews or focus groups, in writing or on audio or video. In any case, you are asking members to define how being a member makes a difference in their lives. That's by far the most powerful marketing tool you could ever have. I'm surprised that most associations don't take this extra step.

I recently sat in a meeting with a member of a chamber of commerce. I asked her why she joined this chamber in particular. Without any prompting, she told me that 80 percent of her business came from chamber members. She added that as a small business owner, she could claim that her chamber membership fed her business, her family, and the families of her employees. Wow! That's amazing value!

The sad part is that the chamber had never asked her to share her story. To say that's a missed opportunity on their part is a huge understatement. It's important to know exactly how your association brings value to your members and be able to articulate how you do it, and it's even better when your members can articulate it for you.

What happens if you're not there? Associations spend a great deal of time and energy on communicating the benefits of membership and all the services and products they provide to their members. This is great—and it's even better when members take part in the marketing of the association. So it may seem odd to think about this, but what would happen if your association didn't exist? Sometimes this information is just as compelling as your member benefits , if not more so. Here are two examples.

I met with someone who worked for an association specializing in a food product. She was really upset because the association was being threatened by declining membership. As she ranted, I was impressed by her passion and terrified by what she said would happen if the association ever went away.

Here's a synopsis of what she said: Don't people realize what we do to protect the industry? We're the ones lobbying at the Hill to make sure our industry is protected! Without us, this food wouldn't be protected. There wouldn't be anyone there to enforce the rules around manufacturing and shelf life. There would be no one to represent this industry, oversee the supply chain, or to make sure the production of this food is safe. As a result, the product would suffer and people would likely get sick.

I perused the association's website, and it says nothing like this. It reads like a textbook, claiming to sponsor health and medical research and serve as an information source to the trade. Sometimes it's better to think about a world where your association doesn't exist because that's where the real passion and truth lies.

Likewise, I recently met with the president of a business association who told me his association was largely responsible for getting the legislative funding needed to build a sports stadium, which resulted in millions of dollars spent in the local economy. I was shocked. I had researched this association inside and out and I had no idea they were involved in this project, much less as a ringleader.

When I mentioned that, the president told me he had decided to keep their participation in the project "under wraps" so as not to steal the spotlight away from the sports team or others who helped on the project. What? As gracious as that may be, it's penny-wise and pound-foolish. This association would have a powerful story to tell its members—and a really compelling reason for members to pay dues.

If this association had not taken the lead on a lobbying effort, the stadium funding likely would not have passed and the local economy would be short a few million dollars. It's okay to toot your own horn. Just don't blow your chance when a great opportunity presents itself.

→ What's the cost-to-value ratio?

Everybody wants more value. The challenging economic climate has forced many associations to ponder how to increase income now. Likewise, your members are questioning the return on investment (ROI) they receive for paying dues.

Demographic shifts must be considered. In associations there are two types of members: givers and takers. Givers willingly pay their dues, volunteer their time, and give of their resources. Unfortunately, most of the givers tend to be from the Baby Boomer generation and are starting to retire their association memberships as they retire from work. Takers, who tend to be from younger generations, say, "I will show up if you can show me value."

When the economy takes a dip, givers may question what they get in return for paying dues. Takers will always question what they get in return for paying dues, regardless of what the economy is doing. As the Boomers phase out of the workplace and your association relies more on Generation X and Y, your association will need to take an open-book approach to dues. This means actually line-iteming what membership benefits are worth.

It comes down to marketing. Many associations fail when communicating dues structures to stakeholders. Oftentimes, they fail to make the vital quantitative (measurable data) as well as qualitative (experiences and outcomes) link between dues dollars and services, benefits, and programs provided.

The steps listed above will help you build a compelling case. To further prove your worth, ask a group of members to provide an accurate estimate of the yearly sustainable dollar value of each of your membership benefits. Start with a comprehensive list of the benefits your association membership provides—from the obvious to the not-so-obvious, including industry-specific training, monthly legislative updates, publicity opportunities, networking, mentoring, product knowledge, credibility, and tax savings.

Next, ask members to put a value on each of the benefits. It may take some time to reach a consensus on each line item, but the numbers should start to add up. For example, most companies would put a high value on industry-specific training—at least $1,000.

Compare this number (the value) to the price of dues and attendance at the association's annual or semi-annual meetings. There should be a substantial difference between the two numbers. This is your cost-to-value ratio.

Here are some examples of how associations use the cost-to-value ratio to their advantage.

The Sacramento chapter president of the **Society for Marketing Professional Services** has an article posted on the chapter's website addressing the cost-to-value ratio that a SMPS membership provides. The article sites the numerous benefits a membership in SMPS offers, providing value in comparison to the price of a membership, which is $355.

To support their cost-to-value argument, the site features a list of the top seven reasons to join, the three reasons why membership in SMPS benefits a company, and member videos and testimonials touting the benefits of membership.

The **Paperboard Packaging Council** actually guarantees a return on membership investment. The association produces a brochure which states, "Membership value will exceed membership costs—we promise." The brochure goes on to highlight all the exclusive benefits a membership in PPC provides.

The **Ohio Restaurant Association** (ORA) takes the guarantee approach a step further. ORA produces an annual Member Value Summary, highlighting all the challenges that were cited in member surveys and the new products, services, and actions ORA implemented to respond to those challenges.

Also, ORA and the **National Restaurant Association** developed a ROI calculator that lets members add up the return on their membership dues themselves. For ORA members, the average value of a membership is $7,300!

Publish that cost-to-value break-down on your association website and in recruitment materials—and you may want to add a synopsis of your association's costs and community investments so members can understand exactly what their dues are funding. This is where the concept of "open book management" comes into play. Younger generations appreciate an organization's efforts to be open and honest and the opportunity to better understand the big picture of organizational operations.

You've now made it easy for members and prospects to justify the dollars necessary to take advantage of membership. You've proven your worth. Even if you are an association that offers free membership, you've still proven your value.

If you find that your cost exceeds your value, then you probably need to restructure your benefits because members won't continue to pay a premium without receiving value in return. If you remain concerned about your value and you want to lower dues, proceed with caution.

Increasing the association's short-term cash flow is usually not a good reason to change your dues structure. It's also not an effective way to build long-term relationships. Changing your dues structure is a tedious process that can take several months to effectively communicate. If you are reconsidering your dues structure, it should be because you want to make it easier for prospects to join, acquire members in new audiences, enable better service, or correct unprofitable equations.

Events throughout history have had the potential to create challenges for associations. Founded as communities with shared values and interests, associations have survived because people needed one another. They prospered because demand was high and competition was minimal. In other words, associations were dominant in the marketplace. As a result, associations have been capable of overcoming war, tragedy, and economic ruin. Their ability to thrive in the face of tragedy gives us hope for the future of associations.

However, technology and demographic shifts will change the course of associations because these two evolutions in and of themselves have altered the way people relate to one another. Today, your association membership is more crucial to your success than ever before. Today, your association is facing challenges unprecedented in history. Today is the day to start rebuilding your dominance.

2

Embracing Change

"When you're finished changing,
you're finished."
Benjamin Franklin

I resigned from a board of directors once. It was an agonizing
decision to make—one that I lost sleep over. I had never quit
anything before. I wasn't raised to be a quitter. My parents made
me see through all my commitments, no matter how miserable I
was.

But as I look back, I didn't resign because I was miserable. I
quit because the board leadership had quit; they had given up
on the association's ability to change, which was essentially a
death sentence. I couldn't associate myself with a leadership that
refused to save a sinking ship. As a board member, it was my duty
to do everything in my power to care for the association. When
I realized that all my efforts to fulfill this important task were
fruitless, I jumped ship.

My area of expertise is in strategic planning and helping
associations plan for membership growth and financial growth.
Along the way, I've worked with associations that were in an
absolute state of panic about their futures. These tend to be the

most at-risk associations. At-risk associations avoid change as long as possible. They wait until the end is staring them in the face.

Leadership of at-risk associations will unknowingly adopt an entitlement syndrome, believing that the problem really isn't as bad as it seems and everything will pan out just fine. Its group mentality says, "Our members have supported us in the past and will continue to support us no matter what."

It's also a "not my fault" mentality. The leaders of at-risk associations often blame someone else for the association's decline. They will claim, "The association management company drove the association downward," or, "We inherited these problems from the previous board."

Associations will also squander limited resources to avoid death. I've worked with more than one association with only six months in reserves, desperate to find a quick-fix solution, yet unwilling to take risks and still clinging to ineffective, outdated programs.

Change is perhaps the most difficult challenge for association leaders to accept. Especially if you're leading an association that's been in existence for 100 years, it can be terrifying to think the association's demise will occur on your watch. So leaders cling to what they know, blame others, throw money at their problems, and desperately hope that something will change the association's fate.

The economic landscape is shifting membership into a downward trend for some associations. The **Credit Union National Association** has been plagued by mergers and economic decline. In 2008, more than one-third of all credit unions operating had participated in at least one merger between 1979 and 2008. In 2011, an industry survey revealed that the biggest challenge for 61 percent of credit unions is attracting new members. In June

2011, CUNA disclosed that a special Affiliation Task Force met to plot ways to halt the CU member slide at leagues. The member drop in leagues is affecting CUNA's ability to provide the same level of programs and services.

Amidst credible contentions that national teacher unions are losing memberships, the **Oklahoma Education Association** lost 707 members during the 2009–2010 year, largely due to the elimination of about 2,000 teaching positions state-wide. According to an article in Tulsa Today, that 707-member loss translates into lost revenue of nearly $300,000 for the union, using an assumption of about $410 per member for annual dues.

Let's face it: These are difficult times for associations. Members want more for less, and associations are struggling to meet members' demands while trying to adapt to changes in technology and demographics. Membership recruitment and retention is more difficult—and more urgent—than ever before. Associations are scrambling to find solutions and flying by the seat of their pants. Nevertheless, associations must be careful not to get too ingrained in the present. (I've worked with associations that are still talking about the *past,* much less the present!) It's imperative that associations start thinking about the future.

Focus on the Future

The failure to anticipate the future will guarantee greater frustration and conflict during decline, which usually occurs during times of reduced financial strength, and that's where most associations are finding themselves right now.

If you're one of the associations that is doing well right now, that's a really, really good sign. In January 2011, I received an email from Stephanie Menning, Vice President of Gas Services at **Midwest Energy Association.** She shared with me this fabulous news:

"MEA has weathered these last few years extremely well. We are flush with cash, are maintaining/growing our membership and after three years of careful planning we're on the path to go national after 106 years as a 15-state regional trade association."

Her email shares a key strategy to her association's success: planning.

Healthy, successful associations are responsive to change. They don't walk around with their eyes closed. They are constantly thinking ahead and moving forward. These associations seek new opportunities, set goals, and carefully plan for their futures. Your best chances of making a successful change occur early on. Whatever you do, don't wait until the last minute to try to save your association. Here's an example of another association that planned for its future and reaped the rewards.

American College of Sports Medicine

In 2003, the American College of Sports Medicine was coasting along with the largest membership in the association's history. However, between 2004 and 2006, the association observed significant losses and didn't realize a net gain in membership again until 2007. In comparison to the net losses of the previous years, this net gain was minimal. ACSM's leaders realized they weren't recruiting enough new members to compensate for the number of members the association was losing. They also realized that their greatest turnover existed among professionals under age 40. The association sought outside help and made significant changes to rebuild its dominance.

The American College of Sports Medicine was a graying organization with a declining membership, so the association set out to make some significant changes.

"We defined change by deciding whether the changes we wanted to make would lead to progress," says Jim Whitehead,

CEO. "Change in and of itself isn't necessarily progress. But we determined up front what we wanted the intended outcomes to be. I think some associations can actually go backward in performance instead of forward because they make changes just for the sake of making changes. We tethered change to progress and that made the difference."

For starters, ACSM changed by concentrating on growth in membership among college students. Student membership was designed to be affordable and offered customized benefits, including access to scholarship information, career-focused webinars, a job center, and a student newsletter. ACSM launched Mentornet, an online mentoring service that uses a profile-matching engine to match mentors with students in similar fields of interests. Within the first month, 75 ACSM members had signed up to participate.

In addition, ACSM introduced a Student Affairs Committee composed of 12 students elected by ACSM regional chapters, a board liaison who is elected by the entire membership, and a staff liaison that coordinates communication and action items. Articles and continuing education programs were added to the website to engage ACSM members in activities year-round—not just in conferences one or two times per year.

ACSM also launched a new Faculty Network to connect with college professors in the association's areas of expertise: sports medicine and exercise science. Adding this new membership category has proven to be highly successful for ACSM. Professors have joined the association, and they serve as ambassadors for ACSM by encouraging their students to join.

Also, the association created two affiliate societies within ACSM: the Clinical Exercise Physiology Association and the

International Association of Worksite Health Promotion. The societies operate like chapters and provide additional resources on two key areas of interest to members. Likewise, when the association was approached by an ever-expanding membership base with diverse backgrounds and interests, ACSM sought out other nonprofits specializing in these sub-specialties and formed partnerships with them.

Have all these changes made a difference for ACSM? Yes! ACSM observed a 13.5 percent increase in membership between 2007 and 2011, especially among students. The association has also seen growth in the number of members taking certification exams, increased media calls and mentions, and increased open rates on the association e-newsletter.

Also in 2010, ACSM successfully took a national program to a global audience and had the largest annual conference attendance in the association's history. "In the last 12 months, we have seen a whole host of positive outcomes in addition to our traditional measurements of success," Whitehead says. "We essentially didn't see a recession for our association."

The leaders' willingness to recognize the association wasn't headed in the right direction and its ability to respond quickly to change made all the difference. "Associations can't just react to change. They're going to have to be proactive. They're going to have to be able to say, 'This is no longer an option.' For ACSM, we were a graying organization and we knew we couldn't survive without engaging young members. We also didn't understand what these generations wanted from ACSM, so we had to be proactive and figure it out," Whitehead says.

Making a Change

There are four responses to change: denial, fear, acceptance, and embracing.

Your association must embrace change or its chances for survival are greatly reduced, if not improbable. Of course, it's easier to keep doing things as you've always done them. In fact, it would be easier to create a brand new association than to change an existing one. When an association is already established, people must unlearn the old values, assumptions, and behaviors before they can learn—and accept—the new ones.

So why change? Amid declining membership, market share, and plummeting revenues, many associations stand frozen in fear or swearing up and down there is nothing different or better that could be done to solve their problems. As they are doing this, they are ensuring their associations' demise. No association is capable of maintaining dominance when it is operating from defiance or fear. Denial and fear are two tickets on the fast train to the middle of nowhere. If your association is already sitting on that train, you must find a way out. Fast.

If you need proof—for yourself, your staff, or your board of directors—there are ways to determine whether change is needed. You can measure your association's expected life span. Here's how.

Association Life Expectancy

1. *First, calculate your association's retention rate.*
   How many members you retain each year is an important indicator of the health of your association, partly because retention costs so much less than recruiting and partly because you want to determine whether retention is going up or down. Ideally, you should run the numbers for the past

five years to see how your association is faring and to identify trends.

To determine your association's retention rate, take the number of renewals, divide it by your total membership (the number eligible to renew) and multiply it by 100 to make it a percentage. If 920 of 1,000 members renew, your retention rate is 92 percent.

The formula is Retention Rate = number of renewals divided by number eligible to renew (100).

2. *Next, calculate your association's loss rate.*
This will determine how many members dropped their memberships this year. Run the numbers for the past five years to see how your association has been faring. To determine your association's loss rate, take the number of dropped members, divide it by your total membership (the number eligible to renew) and multiply it by 100 to make it a percentage.

Here's an example: If 80 members drop out from an eligible renewal base of 1,000, the loss rate is 8 percent. The formula is Loss Rate = number of dropped members divided by number eligible to renew (100).

3. *Then, calculate your turnover.*
This is the most important number. This is your association's life expectancy—the time in which your association will cease to exist if you fail to exceed your loss rate. To determine your association's turnover period in years, divide 100 by your loss rate. For example, with an 8 percent loss rate, it would take 12.5 years to wipe out your membership.

The formula is Turnover Period (years) = 100 divided by Loss Rate (expressed in a percentage).

An eight percent loss rate may not seem like a serious threat, but when you crunch the numbers, you can see that your association can't survive sustained losses. This formula doesn't take into consideration the losses your association is likely to encounter as Baby Boomers retire. As they phase out of the workforce over the next 20 years, associations are going to lose substantial numbers of board members, executives, volunteers, and members.

The following formula will help your association not only identify areas where there will be losses of members with important skills or knowledge but also create a response timeline.

Membership Turnover

Where brain drain is likely to hit first is an important indicator of the future health of your association. When you can measure the loss of Baby Boomers within your association staff and within your membership, you can effectively project your losses and prepare accordingly.

Start with your staff and most invested members (board of directors, committee leaders, long-time volunteers). If you're comfortable distributing a succession planning survey to these people, that's one way to obtain the information. If you're not comfortable with surveying, you can appoint a staff person or consultant to make some educated guesses about member demographics.

In any case, give each person an attrition score of 1 to 5, with 1 denoting a person who isn't likely to leave the association because of retirement for six years or longer, and 5 indicating someone who will be gone within a year. This same process could be used to determine dissatisfaction with the association and the people who are likely to leave, but that's not what you're trying to pinpoint with this particular exercise. You want a better idea about how retirement is likely to affect your association.

I recently conducted a similar exercise for a client. While the staff was fairly young, 90 percent of board members were likely to retire within the next five years. This was a red flag. Furthermore, this association tracked the ages of its members but had never analyzed the data. Imagine the shock when they discovered that 78 percent of their members were eligible to retire in the next 10 years. This was a harsh reality for them, but at least they had the data they needed to make a leap of faith and change their destiny.

Now the association has a plan for recruiting younger members and training them for leadership roles, and it is introducing new technology-based platforms, a national marketing campaign, celebrity endorsements, and programming targeted to young professionals. This association's chances of survival have greatly increased because it acted on problems predicted by projecting its member retirement rate.

Once you've analyzed your own data, you will have a better idea of how quickly your association must change. This just may be the proof your association needs to move forward and make a change.

The next step is to develop a strategy for moving forward. Here's another example of a small organization that made big changes to adapt to future trends, corner a market, and build a thriving association.

In 1983, 15 New England law libraries established a cooperative network, the New England Law Library Consortium (NELLCO). The consortium was driven by the deans of law schools, who saw libraries as cost centers and decided to collaborate to conserve costs. Within a short time, other law libraries were knocking on the door wanting to join the consortium. With no growth plan in place and a lot of anxiety about growth beyond the New England region, NELLCO shied away from change until its leaders realized they were sitting on a potential goldmine. The association made significant changes to grow and build its dominance.

Here's the story.

New England Law Library Consortium

NELLCO launched in 1983 with 15 law libraries as members, each with a representative sitting on the board of directors. In the late 1990s, the association grew to allow a handful of other law libraries not located in New England to join the association. By 2001, NELLCO had 25 members, all with seats on the board of directors. Inquiries from other libraries interested in joining NELLCO started coming in, but there was internal turmoil about whether or not to continue to grow.

Tracy Thompson-Przylucki, executive director, explained that NELLCO didn't have a growth plan because the association didn't start out with intentions to grow. The association was founded on the premise that it would remain an intimate, resource-sharing group. As larger law libraries from throughout the United States started approaching NELLCO about membership, the association was challenged to think about growing from the one membership category that serves on the board to allowing new categories and an entirely new membership model.

The concept of change was not taken lightly. "We actually had a scheduled debate—one side took the no-growth stance and one took the pro-growth," Thompson-Przylucki says. While NELLCO's potential growth posed tremendous opportunity, it also posed many concerns, such as losing the value members had gained through collegiality and growing too large to effectively manage the association. In the end, the benefits outweighed the risks. NELLCO's board decided they needed to be responsive to the needs of their industry.

"Ultimately, the pro-growth side won because no one else was doing what we were doing and libraries were knocking on our door," Thompson-Przylucki says. Opportunity knocked, and NELLCO answered by creating different categories of membership and opening itself up for growth opportunities. Soon, NELLCO was receiving inquiries from outside the United States and introduced another membership category for these libraries.

As of 2010, NELLCO had grown to include 25 full members, 78 affiliate members from 33 states across the United States, and 10 international affiliate members from four countries. Every outcome to the change in NELLCO's membership model has been positive. NELLCO has been able to tap into more opportunity—new projects, new technology, new staff—because it has more infrastructure financially.

Thompson-Przylucki says her advice to other associations contemplating a change would be to put people first. "People are dedicated to their associations. You don't want to alienate people who have been there from the outset. Be really careful, thoughtful, and communicative of issues. Taking the time to do that ultimately made our transition successful. Even the people who were skeptical at first now can say we made the right decision."

In the end, Thompson-Przylucki believes NELLCO has succeeded at building their association because the leadership was open to change.

Ohio State Medical Association

The Ohio State Medical Association experienced many of the same challenges related to change. Its motivation to change was not based on growth initiatives; rather, it was the direct result of changes within the industry.

Founded in 1846, Ohio State Medical Association serves a vital role in Ohio, advising state departments on health issues and giving Ohio's physicians a voice in legislative issues. The association represents 20,000 physicians, residents, medical students, and practice managers.

Nevertheless, the historic association has been challenged in recent years.

David Owens, senior director and chief marketing officer, explained that the association started to lose leverage with members of all types. For example, hospitals have their own lobbyists now and physicians don't think they need the advocacy an OSMA membership provides.

On the other end of the spectrum, independent and small clinic physicians are juggling the bureaucratic burdens placed on them by insurance companies and government, and medical liability insurance is increasingly more expensive. While these physicians saw value in what an OSMA membership provides, they were struggling to afford membership. There's tremendous pricing sensitivity for physicians right now, and dues are more than $500.

As a state medical society, an OSMA membership included membership in the physician's county medical society. In 2009, OSMA proposed a new membership option at its annual meeting. Under the revised terms, a physician would have the choice to be a member of both the OSMA and his/her county medical society, of only the OSMA, or of only the county medical society.

The proposed membership change needed a 59 percent approval vote; it didn't pass. But OSMA wasn't giving up on the idea of implementing change. For starters, OSMA convinced its current board to approve adding six new seats (ex-officio officers). "We wanted the new positions to be representative of large hospital institutions, as well as young physicians and academics," Owens said. "We're trying to better represent the physician population on our council rather than continuing leadership by people who are elected by a rite of passage in traditional mechanisms. We're hoping new faces and new thinking will help the organization think smarter and be more strategic for the future."

OSMA also launched an extensive marketing campaign titled "I belong." The campaign featured member testimonials and all the compelling reasons they belong to OSMA, using statements like, "I belong because I'm a practitioner, not a politician." The campaign worked. Within a single week, OSMA enrolled 50 new members.

During the 2011 OSMA annual meeting, the revised membership resolution passed—165 years after the association was founded. It took time and persistence, but the change was imperative for OSMA to continue to provide value and remain relevant in the changing environment of health care delivery. "A lot of associations have ideas they can't implement because of leadership—usually the old guard that doesn't want to change—and frankly because we are nonprofits and the culture isn't set up to be competitive. So you have to show people why they have to change, why things need to be different, why we have to be more efficient," Owens says. "Those associations that can't change and be progressive will fall out. They will become irrelevant and once they become irrelevant, no one will want to join them."

In each of these success stories, associations weren't necessarily prepared to change, or even open to it at first, but they were responsive to it.

Whether your association is experiencing a decline in membership, has an aging membership, or is resisting growth, being responsive to your association's needs is usually indicative of your ability to be responsive to change. Such associations will survive. Their leaders aren't prolonging the inevitable, ignoring trends, blaming others, being indecisive, or taking other actions that jeopardize their associations' futures.

Change can be a challenge. But change is also an opportunity; an opportunity to take the lead, to grow, to succeed. By all means, don't fear change! Embrace it. It's your only path to the future.

3

Offering Better Benefits

"Strive not to be a success,
but rather to be of value."
Albert Einstein

My biggest pet peeve when it comes to membership associations is when I shell out big bucks for a membership and then I still have to pay for everything else to be able to actually use my membership.

Nickel-and-diming is a strategy that associations could get by with in the past, but it's not going to work anymore. In the past, a membership could buy you nothing but a listing in the membership directory and a discount on car rentals. Indeed, when your association is dominant in the marketplace, demand for membership is high, competition is minimal, and you can name your price. However, associations have been losing their grip on the marketplace since around 2005.

First, when younger generations were being recruited for membership, they were the first to really question the value a membership brings and to demand a return on their membership investments.

Then the economy took a nosedive, and everyone began demanding more return on their investments. Throw technology into the mix, and now it's possible for your members to access all kinds of professional development and networking—most of it for free!

The tables have turned. Demand is weak, competition is up, and your association's value is going down like a bad real estate investment. There's only one way out of this mess: outcome-based member benefits.

This leads to my second pet peeve: when associations list the features of membership instead of the outcomes. Networking opportunities and a listing in the membership directory are two popular benefits associations like to list. I wouldn't recommend listing these as main benefits because they really don't carry any substantial value. I could access networking opportunities with your members without purchasing a membership, and a listing in the directory has a very small chance of actually driving more business to my doorstep.

In contrast, your association should focus on the outcomes of membership. A membership listing and networking are features. It's like saying a tissue is white. It's obvious. If the tissue company tells you that by using its tissue to blow your nose, you can help stop the spread of germs, that's an outcome. Now you can better understand the difference between this tissue and all other tissues on the market and you feel good about making that purchase.

So rather than call a membership listing and networking benefits, wouldn't it be better to use an outcome-based approach and state that a membership in your association leads to business contacts that can result in new business opportunities? Even better, do some research and quantify those new business opportunities. When you can tout that 60 percent of members report their membership has resulted in new business opportunities, you have actual proof that your membership is valuable.

It's the association's job not only to provide members with benefits but also to adequately communicate and market those benefits. Your members are looking for benefits that add value to their businesses and lives, not merely a basket of products and services.

Value Mistakes

Most of the associations that are struggling to grow membership fall into one of the following categories. Their common diagnosis: failure to deliver value to members.

1. Scrooge Associations

These associations are notorious for nickel-and-diming their members. These associations may not even realize the error of their ways, but they tend to charge too much and give too little. It's difficult to distinguish the benefits of joining the association because a member still has to pay for every product, program, and service the association offers.

2. Milk Associations

These associations have lost sight of what a membership means. Membership offers little exclusivity or access. It's difficult to distinguish between the benefits of joining the association and just paying to attend the events or purchase services a la carte. In other words, why pay for the whole cow when you can pay for just the milk?

3. Antique Associations

These associations have been in the marketplace for many years and have renowned brands. In recent years they have declined simply because they are no longer relevant. Their benefits were meaningful in the past, but they have been unable to adapt to the needs of today's audiences.

Perhaps you recognize the characteristics of your own association in one of these categories and you're wondering what to do about it. It all comes down to value. Member benefits are your association's one and only asset, the key to building a dominant and financially stable organization. Here's how to flip your fortunes by turning value mistakes into valuable memberships.

Turning a Scrooge into a Trump

I recently consulted with an association that was perplexed about why membership was going down. The president explained to me he had lowered the cost of all their programming, realizing that members wouldn't pay a premium price for events in a tough economy. I agreed this was a good idea. Then I asked him about the cost of membership. My analysis had shown this association's membership was priced higher than any of the associations in the industry. Was he willing to lower that price?

His answer was no. He explained that a switch in dues pricing is a difficult tactic to implement and once you lower your price you can't bump it back up. Again, I agreed. My line of questioning was intentional. Because I wanted him to fully comprehend where he had made an error in his rationale, then I asked him what he was doing to increase the *value* of the membership. He went back to the topic of pricing. I told him that I wasn't referring to pricing any longer, I was referring to value. I explained that the membership had simply lost its value and needed to be increased—not through a price fluctuation—but a change in the actual deliverables.

Most association executives get lost in financial numbers. This is understandable because the executives want to make sure they keep the budget operating in the black. Any decrease in membership and their first knee-jerk reaction is to refer to the budget. I was terrible at math in school. So I've learned how to analyze data from other points of view. Here's my advice: Number-crunching is critical to maintaining your budget, but if you are losing members left and right, you need to get your head out of the budget and into the minds of your membership.

The number one reason members join an association is because they believe that association will help them solve a problem. Right now, the number one problem most people are facing is likely related to their finances. The economy has forced people out of jobs, cut into their savings, and jeopardized their futures. This means two things:

First and foremost, your members don't want to be nickel-and-dimed. If they join your association or renew their dues, they want that money to pay for access to much more than a listing in the directory and a discount on car rental.

Second, your members want your association to help them solve their problems. Right now, this means providing programming and services related to helping them find jobs, make money, and feel good about their futures.

In the example I shared above, the association was offering very few programs or services to respond to current financial issues, it offered absolutely nothing of value for free that was included in the membership price, and the few social events they hosted each year came with a hefty price tag. It's no surprise that membership was declining!

In stark contrast to this association, I later met with another association that was doing everything right.

Associated Builders and Contractors of Metro Washington had hosted a series of programs addressing industry projections and providing tools to help their member companies compete. Recognizing that workforce development was a concern for their industry, they also provided a nine-month series focused on leadership training.

In addition, they hosted a lobster bake that was free for their members. This social event was organized by the association to show appreciation for their members, build fellowship among the membership, and make members feel good about their continued involvement in the association.

Membership was up, even though this association's industry had been hard hit by the economy. This shows that members will continue to pay dues, no matter what the circumstances, so long as your association provides them with value.

Billionaire real estate mogul Donald Trump always tells people the secret to success is to "do what you love." In his book, *Think Big and Kick A** in Business and Life* (Collins; October, 2007), Trump writes, "Don't think about how you can make money. Instead think about what you can produce or what service you can offer that is valuable and useful to people in your community."

Bottom line: If you're a Scrooge Association, you have to stop counting your coins and start thinking about ways you can help your members. Add to your list of member benefits and stop charging members extra for everything. As the old saying goes, you will get what you give. If you want to get more members, give them more reasons to join.

Turning a Glass of Milk into a Cash Cow

A few years ago, some association somewhere decided to start opening the doors to nonmembers. The idea was that if nonmembers had access to the same pricing or just slightly higher pricing as the members had for events, products, and services, the result would be more revenue. Nonmembers would preview the association, fall in love with it, and make the decision to join. And if they didn't join, at least the association was getting their money.

This a la carte approach may have seemed like a genius idea for membership conversion, but for most associations the concept backfired. It backfired because most associations didn't offer enough membership value to entice prospects to convert into members. Therefore, prospective members failed to see the value in purchasing a full membership when they could just as easily, and more affordably, access the few events or member benefits they wanted one at a time.

Milk Associations give too much away or offer too little membership value, so they struggle to get people to buy the cow (pay for a membership) because it's easier for them to just buy the milk (programs, events, and other services a la carte).

I belonged to a business association for several years. The association hosted one event each month and the annual gala drew in great speakers and an audience of more than 600 people. Members paid to attend each of these monthly programs and the annual gala in addition to their annual dues.

A couple years into my membership, I suddenly realized that my membership didn't pay for any benefits. Outside of the programming, the association didn't offer any other member benefits. Not one! The association's area of expertise had become event planning! Why pay for a membership when I could just pay to attend the events? I wasn't the only one who noticed the lack of benefits and the association experienced a sharp decline in membership within an 18-month timeframe.

Even with people attending events, the association found itself struggling to get by without the dues revenue. The association needed dues to sustain operations and made a horrible mistake by cutting out or neglecting its membership benefits to focus exclusively on events.

If you're a Milk Association, you are likely making the mistake of tracking program ROI (return on investment) instead of tracking member ROI. This means your association spends a great deal of time and resources on planning events and the association's budget relies heavily on the income generated from those events from members and non-members alike. However, outside of programming there are few additional streams of revenue and few member benefits. As a result, you have a high percentage of people who attend the events or purchase services a la carte but do not join the association. It's the equivalent of selling glasses of milk rather than selling cows.

There's nothing wrong with this approach, but it is misleading when you are operating under the guise of a membership association because it doesn't have a member-centric strategy and it doesn't hold much promise for your association's long-term success.

In contrast to programming ROI, membership ROI is a long-term investment strategy—a cash cow, if you will. People pay their membership dues and continue to invest in the association throughout the year because they see value in everything the association has to offer.

A membership ROI-driven association is completely focused on delivering value and attending to the needs of its members. Additional streams of revenue are built into the association, all which are focused on addressing the needs and interests of the members. Also, members receive a return on their dues investment with access to valuable information, opportunities, and resources. A successful membership-focused association has a growing membership and high retention and participation rates.

Membership ROI means delivering a variety of meaningful member benefits. It also means that when you do offer programming and resources to non-members, you charge them a higher price. You don't want to go to extremes and charge prices that make it impossible for prospects to engage. That's not the point and it's against Association Law, to boot. The point is to avoid being an a la carte association that gives everything away to focus on building in more value, opportunity, and access for your members. Membership must have its benefits. That's the only way your association can successfully retain members and recruit members.

If your association is really struggling to recruit and retain members, you may need to shift your focus from delivering exceptional one-offs for just anyone to delivering exceptional, year-round value to your members.

As the old saying goes, why buy the cow when you can get the milk for free? In other words, membership must have its benefits or your association risks losing the farm.

Turning an Antique into a Precious Commodity

Antique Associations are challenged the most. Their legacies are both a blessing and a curse. Much like an old house, Antique Associations have tremendous, awe-inspiring character and influence.

These associations are rooted in tradition, have loyal members, and boast a culture that's nearly impenetrable. They have reputable brands and have prospered in years past. The leaders of Antique Associations take great pride in what they've built. Nevertheless, their foundations are falling apart.

For Antique Associations, change is a foreign, even unwelcome, concept. The leadership has done everything in its power to preserve the association's traditions, which have been unable to withstand the current winds of change. As a result, these associations have struggled to stay relevant amid an aging leadership and declining membership.

I have closely observed two Antique Associations divided by change. In each situation, a heated discussion took place at the association's annual conference where a small group of people was rallying loudly in favor of change, while the majority was voicing opposition to change.

One of these associations tried to instill change, but they were far too late in doing so. The association folded after 90 years, unable to keep members or resources intact. The other association, founded in the late 1800s, is barely holding on.

In the near future, other associations may go by the wayside, an entire era of history lost simply because they can't adapt to change. The changes are the direct result of the three major influences in society mentioned in Chapter One: rapidly-changing technology, demographic shifts, and economic recovery. These three things have changed what your members want and need. Our values as a society have changed, and associations need to be responsive to these changes in order to remain relevant.

If your association falls into the Antique category, you must make a change. Now. The marketplace is competitive and time is running out. An Antique Association must take measures to stay relevant, and that starts with an analysis of the association's member benefits. If your association hasn't updated its list of member benefits in several years, by today's standards, that's the kiss of death.

Your association's value is directly based on its ability to respond to your members' needs. When you are unable to respond to member needs, your association's value goes down and you will inevitably observe a decline in membership and revenue.

Bottom line: Your association has already made history. If your association wants its legacy to live on, there is no past. There's only future. You must build your association with the future in mind.

Member Benefits Formula

Regardless of where you fall on the continuum—Scrooge, Milk, or Antique Association—the secret to your association's success hinges on one thing: member benefits. When you can identify and deliver on what your members want and need from your association, you will have a very valuable commodity to offer and you will rebuild your dominance.

Members join your association because they believe in your ability to solve a problem for them. They renew their membership when you are successful at solving the problem, engage them in a community, and make them feel good about being a member. So a successful membership benefits formula is equally practical and emotional.

One of the best examples of member benefit packages is the one provided by the **National Association of Independent Life Brokerage Agencies**. This association offers so many member benefits it's hard to imagine any independent life brokerage agency passing up the opportunity to join. I counted 27 member benefits—and not once is networking listed!

Here's a sampling of what NAILBA offers its members, as stated in the NAILBA Member Benefits Guide:

- Free registration for a NAILBA member agency principal to attend NAILBA's annual conferences: FOCUS (a $700 value) and the Annual Meeting (a $1,400 value);

- NAILBA's magazine, which highlights current developments in the insurance and wholesale brokerage field;

- Agency Resources, a section on the website that provides how-to information to brand and promote benefits and services to agents;

- On-line Legislative Action Center, where members can communicate directly with their Congressional representative on the issues that impact their agency;

- NAILBA University, providing members substantial discounts on many educational offerings, free educational tools and resources for their agency, and customizable agency promotions;

- Password-protected online address book of key personnel at the major life insurance companies as well as vendors and life settlement companies;

- Referral fees when agents enter the name of the NAILBA member agency that referred them on the NAILBA website;

- Sales Quenchers partnership providing NAILBA's agents sales training tips sent directly to their mobile phones at a significant discount, plus a 15 percent discount on additional sales consulting and training programs;

- Toshiba America partner program, which offers NAILBA members significant discounts on the purchase or lease of leading electronics products;

- WebCE, a nationwide provider specializing in continuing education courses for licensed insurance professionals and financial planners, provides NAILBA member agencies distance learning courses at a discounted rate; and

- An exclusive Errors & Omissions insurance program specifically tailored to meet the needs of NAILBA members (independent insurance agents).

Obviously, NAILBA is really tapped into solving its members' needs, providing them with ample opportunities to advance their careers and cut costs. That's the problem-solving, practical part of the value-building equation.

As for the emotional side, it is evident from this list of benefits that NAILBA goes above and beyond to express gratitude and genuine concern for their members. The motive of nearly every member benefit listed is to benefit NAILBA members by bringing them more success careerwise, revenuewise, and otherwise.

The key difference between good associations and great associations is their willingness to go above and beyond the normal order of doing business to meet their members' needs. Sometimes those needs can't be predicted. Consider what the Moore County Chamber of Commerce did when the economy in their region hit rock-bottom. Here's how it invested $25 and made it into a small fortune.

Moore County Chamber of Commerce

Moore County is a relatively rural North Carolina county. The county's main industry is leisure travel. It is home to Pinehurst Resort, host of numerous golf tournaments, including the 2014 U.S. Open.

At the end of 2008, the housing market started to slow significantly and the resort businesses started suffering as well. Patrick Coughlin, Chamber president and CEO, said he knew his small chamber of 825 members had to do something to help its local businesses.

The board decided that if a membership lapsed any longer than 60 days, Coughlin and other chamber staff would meet with the business manager one-on-one and ask, "What can we do to keep you? What can you afford?" In some cases it was $25. What's admirable about this effort is that Coughlin worried less about the Chamber's revenue and ability to survive than he did about helping the Chamber's members.

"It's not only about the dollar. Our business is to make our members more successful because they are members of the chamber. We knew it would be tough but we also knew it would return in spades. We were investing in tomorrow, not today," Coughlin says.

Indeed, as the economy started to bounce back, the members went above and beyond to express their gratitude to Moore County Chamber. Membership stayed stable and nondues revenue increased as participation in Chamber events increased. Two gold level sponsors moved up to platinum level sponsors, making the decision to reallocate all their advertising budgets to the Moore County Chamber.

Coughlin said the decision to accept reduced dues was the best decision his association could have made. "There's a real attachment to our Chamber now—even more than before. We have increased the level of credibility and trust in our organization because we were able to go to our businesses and say, 'Hey, we understand and we're here to help.'"

The **South Metro Regional Chamber of Commerce,** serving the southern region of Dayton, Ohio, boasts on the organization's website that their member benefits are "ever changing." This is a great way to showcase your dedication to your members as a responsive, needs-based association. After all, once your members stop needing you, there's no reason for your association to exist.

Focus on the Future

This book is about changing membership models, and you can't rethink your membership model without also rethinking your member benefits. Member benefits are the be-all, end-all of your association. Regardless of what your membership model is, if you don't have a compelling reason for members to join or renew, your association doesn't stand a chance of survival. And you need to offer member benefits that are especially appealing to a young audience.

Most associations have excelled at recruiting and retaining Baby Boomers—and remain almost entirely governed by Baby Boomers—but have struggled to engage the next generation of members, leaders, and volunteers. By the way, you don't have to be an Antique Association to be grappling with this issue. I recently spoke with leaders of an association that was formed just two years ago and they already recognized they were failing miserably at engaging young members!

The United States is on the brink of the largest shift in human capital in history. Most of our nation's companies, government, and nonprofit organizations are vastly unprepared for the loss of their leadership and most loyal talent.

This challenge will be addressed in greater detail in the next chapter, but it's worth pointing out here that different generations have different expectations of an association membership. Their values are different, which means the benefits each generation perceives as valuable are also different.

Your association must address the wants and needs of the under-45 crowd because these people could not care less about your association's history, insurance discounts, and annual conference. Your association needs to know what younger generations do care about because without them your association will struggle to survive.

So, here's what you must know. The values of Generations X (1965-1981) and Y (1982-1995) tend to be focused on three primary objectives: the opportunity to lead, the opportunity to learn, and the opportunity to make a difference. Another way of describing their key drivers is this: Younger generations (individuals age 46 and younger) will invest in a membership if, and only if, the membership benefits them personally and professionally and also benefits their community or industry.

Let's break these values down into actual benefits.

1. Leadership

Why is it only a handful of associations actually give leadership roles to younger members? If you're thinking to yourself, "We tried that already and they didn't want to lead," then there was a flaw in your approach.

Allow me to clarify. Young professionals want to be given the opportunity to lead, but they won't jeopardize their personal happiness to do so. This is a critical difference between Baby Boomers and Generations X and Y. Baby Boomers will sit on a board of directors year after year because it's the right thing to do. Younger generations will not.

One association asked me why they couldn't get young people to sit on the board. Further investigation revealed this association held board meetings that were several days long and allowed its board members to renew their terms for a maximum term of 11 years. Eleven years! I'm a Gen Xer and just thinking about an 11-year board term makes my skin crawl!

Xers and Ys will sit on a board for a short time with the intention of doing something that makes a visible difference. To them, leadership is not sitting in endless meetings, engaging in lengthy discussions, and renewing a board term year after year. They want to get in, roll up their sleeves, and make something happen. By their definition, leadership should be an enjoyable, rewarding experience with real outcomes and recognition for their efforts.

When boiled down to actual member benefits, consider adding the following:

- Leadership training for young professionals interested in board service and/or the pursuit of leadership roles within their careers;

- Short-term leadership opportunities, such as organizing a service project or leading a task force;

- The opportunity for young professionals to sit on your association's board (but be open to redefining what board service actually means);

- Recognition for emerging leaders and outstanding young members or volunteers, such as profiles in your newsletter or on your blog and the distribution of awards.

2. Learning

The 1970s introduced 30 years of massive layoffs in corporate America. Generations X and Y watched their parents and relatives get laid off, down-sized, or merged at a moment's notice. Based on historical occurrences combined with what I've read in numerous articles addressing the job market outlook by generation, I've come to the conclusion that Generations X and Y are the first generations to have never known job security. They live in constant fear of losing their jobs.

Not surprising, young professionals actively seek the opportunity to learn new skills. They want to continually expand and hone their skill-sets in case they do lose their jobs. In addition, each generation is better educated than the generation that comes before them. Today's young professionals are well-educated, fast learners, and capable of multi-tasking. They are easily bored and readily seek new challenges.

Taking this need into consideration, associations would be smart to expand their professional development offerings, but avoid making these critical mistakes: Don't limit your professional development to in-person events and don't put a hefty price tag on it. Remember, these people are juggling their careers while raising children, taking classes, and caring for aging relatives, all while paying for mortgages, day care bills, and student debt.

They are extremely pressed for time and money, so offer your members a variety of ways to access this valuable training and make sure it's at a competitive price. Better yet, offer these courses for no additional cost as a member benefit.

Examples of professional development member benefits include:

- Webinars, recorded for download at a later time, providing additional training on a topic of interest;

- Video or audio recordings of all association programs available on the association site for future download;

- Podcasts featuring case studies, helpful information, or tips on a topic of interest;

- Mentoring programs that actively partner young members with established members;

- Round-table small group discussions that allow for significant learning opportunities and relationship-building; and

• Self-guided certification program available via a combination of web-based programming, in-person programming, and other requirements.

Some employers may pay for their employees' membership dues and member programming. However, your association needs to be aware that fewer employers are covering membership costs.

In March 2011, the Philadelphia Business Journal published an article about how bar association membership had dropped on a local and national level because there are fewer working lawyers to pay dues and fewer law firms willing to pay for their lawyers to obtain memberships.

The article noted that the American Bar Association had observed a 7 percent decline between 2007 and 2010. Likewise, the Philadelphia Bar Association (PBA) had suffered a net loss of about 7 percent of its regular dues-paying members. The decline was offset by PBA's increase in specialized, lower-rate memberships for government and public service lawyers and students.

3. Making a Difference

The Baby Boomers, sometimes referred to as the "Me Generation," were raised to aspire for the corner office, title of president or CEO, and the nice salary that accompanied such prestige. Indeed, the Boomers are loyal members and volunteers, but some would argue that Boomers want to be active in these roles to influence change and sit on the board of directors.

Along comes Generations X and Y, and salary and prestige take a backseat to work-life balance and working for an ethical organization. Suddenly, we have generations asking to leave the office early to attend their children's soccer games or inquiring in interviews about the organization's service projects and socially conscious policies.

The ways Generations X and Y want to work and whom they choose to work for carry over into their decision-making process with memberships. These are generations that want to know their participation in your association can literally make a difference in the world. Suddenly, the idea of a transactional membership—giving money to your association to access programming and services—doesn't hold much appeal to 120 million Americans. You are now challenged to make a membership in your association beneficial to people other than just your members.

Examples of socially conscious member benefits include:

- Organized fundraisers or a portion of all dues being directed to community or industry needs;

- Service projects that are both tangible and visible, allowing members the opportunity to engage, volunteer, and make a difference; and

- Environmentally-friendly business practices and opportunities.

One final note on this topic, make sure your community outreach efforts support your association's mission. For example, the **National Christmas Tree Association** gives Christmas trees to military members and their families. The **American Bankers Association** hosts Teach Children to Save Day each year and their members donate time in the schools teaching various savings education programs. If your causes are supportive of your association's mission, it will create more visibility for your association and substantially more value in your membership offer.

Member Benefits Matrix

ASAE & The Center's research study, *The Decision to Join* (2007), details the motivations behind an individual's decision to join— or not to join—a professional association. The report surveyed 16,944 association members nationwide. One chapter in *The Decision to Join* details generational factors of this decision. In the survey, respondents were asked a series of questions about the importance of and satisfaction with both personal benefits and benefits to their entire field.

Generational differences were evident throughout the report's findings. For example, on the topic of "access to career information and employment opportunities," Generation Y scored this personal benefit very high, but their associations' delivery on the benefit as failing to meet expectations. On several related topics, Generation Y indicated higher performance/delivery gaps than older generations.

Likewise, the category "supporting student education and entry into the field" is particularly noteworthy because while Generation Y gave it a negative rating, all other generations gave it a positive rating. Also, Generation Y listed this benefit as the most important, while the other age groups ranked it seventh. Obviously, the generational perspective is significant and influential. You must be able to analyze your association's offerings through the eyes of your youngest members and adjust accordingly.

If you want to measure the success of your membership benefits, use the matrix below to chart your progress. The goal is to identify whether each member benefit your association offers meets your association's objectives. The most successful member benefits will solve a problem or effectively deliver a positive experience or emotion. As you work on overcoming challenges and positioning your benefits, be sure to add benefits that appeal to the values of younger generations.

Benefits Matrix

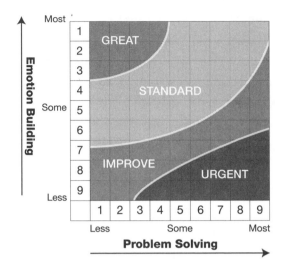

Regardless of what your association is currently offering or may offer in the future, you should consistently measure the potential of all your member benefits. You must ensure your association can be responsive to the needs of its membership, and the needs of the membership are continually changing. Survey members or host focus groups regularly to keep your finger on the pulse of any changing needs among your membership. Nothing can replace the open, honest feedback you receive from members.

Your association's leadership can also use this matrix to measure the success of your benefits. You want to make sure your benefits continually meet the core needs of your membership. Your deliverables may change, but the core needs of your membership will never change. We all join associations wanting a problem solved and we all want the experience to be positive, ultimately resulting in relationship-building opportunities.

Here's how to use the Member Benefits Matrix:

First, give each member benefit a score, on a scale of 1 to 9, for its ability to solve a problem.

Nine Point Problem-Solving Scale

Most Important
(1) Benefit solves a crucial problem for nearly all members—key reason why members join.
(2) Benefit solves an important problem for nearly all members.
(3) Benefit solves an important problem for 70 percent or more of members.

Some Importance
(4) Benefit solves a problem for 50 to 70 percent of members.
(5) Benefit solves a problem for some members, but it is not unique to this association.
(6) Benefit solves a problem for 30 to 50 percent of members.

Less Important
(7) Benefit solves a problem for less than 30 percent of members.
(8) Benefit rarely comes into members' consideration or use.
(9) Benefit never comes into members' consideration or use.

Next, give each member benefit a score, on a scale of 1 to 9, for its ability to deliver positive experiences and emotions.

Nine Point Emotion-Building Scale

Most Important
(1) Benefit consistently delivers a positive experience—key reason why members join or renew.
(2) Benefit delivers a positive experience for nearly all members.
(3) Benefit delivers a positive experience for 70 percent or more of members.

Somewhat Important
(4) Benefit delivers a positive experience for 50 to 70 percent of members.
(5) Benefit delivers a positive experience for some members, but it is not unique to this association.
(6) Benefit delivers a positive experience for 30 to 50 percent of members.

Less Important

    (7) Benefit delivers a positive experience for less than 30
        percent of members.

    (8) Benefit rarely comes into members' consideration or use.

    (9) Benefit never comes into members' consideration or use.

Next, plot the two numbers on the matrix. If you gave your membership directory listing a 9 on problem-solving and an 8 on relationship-building, you would place a single dot on the matrix. The dot would appear in the far right column, just above the 9 on the problem-solving scale and up two squares for placement in the eighth row on the emotional scale. This dot would fall into the "urgent" section of the matrix, which indicates this benefit isn't valuable to members whatsoever. It should be eliminated or revised into something valuable. Once you do this exercise, your association leaders can begin to comprehend where your benefits are falling short and could actually lead to decline in membership and revenue. Plus, your association will be well-equipped to modify and measure its member benefits. I can't emphasize enough the importance of making sure your benefits meet the needs of your membership. Benefits are the difference between a good association and a great one. They can also be the difference between success and failure.

I've worked with associations that have painstakingly adopted new technology, customer service techniques, and logos; hired and fired staff; cut costs or raised costs; and done everything possible to try to reverse declines in membership and revenue. I even came across an association that was bribing people to get them to join! Before you do something you really regret, take a serious look at what you offer. Then ask if membership in your organization is the most valuable, exclusive, problem-solving, people-loving membership you can offer.

4

Furthering Your Reach

"The future belongs to those who
prepare for it today."
Malcolm X

Membership associations are like pizza parlors. I read
somewhere that three fourths of Americans like pizza. Likewise,
according to Pew Research Center, 74 percent of Americans
belong to at least one association. However, if you're in the one
fourth of Americans that don't like pizza, bear with me. I do have
a point to make.

For a really long time, associations have been serving pizza.
In other words, associations have mastered how to deliver
products, services, and events that really appeal to one audience
in particular. The Baby Boomers love the pizza that associations
serve, and in most cases they are the ones frequenting the pizza
parlors and eating all the pizza as well as managing the pizza-
making process and restaurant operations, and possibly even
making the pizza themselves!

Now you have people coming into your restaurant asking what
else is available. Maybe they don't like pizza or they didn't grow
up eating pizza. Maybe they're hoping for something in addition

to pizza. These new consumers tend to be younger. Their unique interests, needs, wants, and expectations have left some Boomers thinking these consumers are self-centered, demanding, and foolish for wanting something other than the fantastic pizza they've made.

Suddenly, as the owner of the pizza parlor, you see new customers storming off in frustration. While management complains that new customers are needed, they certainly aren't serving anything other than pizza. So what do you do? Do you stop serving pizza altogether? Or do you continue to serve only pizza?

Neither. If your association expects to grow membership, even sustain membership, it can't abandon its traditions, but it also can't ignore the opportunity to introduce new members and member benefits.

The U.S. Census Bureau and Bureau of Labor Statistics both predict that by 2015, Baby Boomers will cede the majority of the workforce to Generation Y. It will be the largest shift in human capital in history. Contemplate the significance of that shift. Most membership associations remain almost entirely governed and supported by the Baby Boomer generation. Most associations are still struggling to engage Generation X (currently ages 30 to 46), much less Generation Y (ages 16 to 29).

Can you fathom the world workforce influenced by people in their 20s and early 30s? The Baby Boomer generation has been in power for so long, it's difficult to imagine our corporations, government, schools, nonprofits, and just about every industry being influenced by younger generations. Can you picture your association with Generation Y at the helm? Can you picture 20-somethings at your programs and using your services? And if Gen Ys aren't already highly engaged in your association, do you have a plan for engaging them within the next four years?

The very thought of the shift and your association's ability to adjust to it is enough to make some association executives feel like throwing in the towel. Of course, the less prepared your association is, the more nerve-wracking this topic is likely to be. As an association, there are measures you can take to effectively engage younger generations without alienating the most loyal generations. But if you continue to perceive this pending shift as an insurmountable challenge, all the tips in the world aren't going to help. So roll up your sleeves, and get started on building a highly successful, multigenerational membership model.

The New Recruits

One of the key components of any growth plan is a thorough understanding of the target market. You must know who is most likely to buy your product and why and must plan how you will reach them.

Herein lies the first challenge. Most associations know exactly how to provide value to Baby Boomers and how to market to Baby Boomers, but they have failed miserably at providing value for and marketing to other generations.

In my 2007 book *The New Recruit: What Your Association Needs to Know About X, Y, & Z*, I said:

> Generations X and Y have completely different values, interests, needs, and wants from the generations before them. Their worldview, their priorities—everything about them is different as a result of their social experiences.
>
> Generations X and Y will not respond to the recruiting efforts of the past. An entirely new approach is required. That's why I refer to the younger generations as New Recruits.
>
> There's no such thing as a quick-fix solution here. A membership association can't just go out and launch a blog and expect the younger generations to come running. Everything about the membership association has to change....

There are two types of associations evolving now. The Boomer-centric associations will refuse to change or fear change. These are the associations that are considered endangered species and likely will be extinct by the year 2020.

The New Recruit associations realize the need to recruit and retain younger members and invites younger generations in to help them make the change. These are the associations that will succeed and survive."

Four years later, and associations have made minimal progress in engaging the New Recruits. Why has progress been so difficult? I suspect that one of two things is happening: either associations don't fully understand the needs of their target market or associations don't fully understand the potential of their target market. Or maybe it's some of both.

Target Market Needs

I gave a presentation a few years ago at an ASAE Great Ideas Conference. Someone in the audience vehemently argued that there was no such thing as generational differences. I felt like I was on Candid Camera. Why did this person attend a break-out to learn more about generational differences if he didn't believe generational differences existed in the first place? Let me assure you, generational differences do exist. Scientifically and socially, there is ample proof that the generations differ from one another in their habits, needs, values, wants, interests, and expectations.

I think where people get confused is thinking that generational differences are merely age differences. Think about it. We're all a little more footloose and fancy-free in our twenties. As we age, we gain more wisdom and responsibility, get tired more easily, and approach life differently. The behavioral differences between a 20-year-old and 60-year-old are age differences. However, the decision to join (or not to join) an association isn't an age difference. It's a generational difference.

How do I know this to be true? Just take a look at Generation X—the oldest are 46 and associations are still struggling to engage them. This generation is nearing middle-age and they still aren't "joiners." The decision to join an association isn't something you grow into alongside mortgage payments and diaper changing. The decision to join isn't the result of wisdom or maturity; it's rooted in our most basic needs and wants.

Many, many association executives make the mistake of thinking that younger generations aren't joining their association because they haven't grown into it yet. "Just give it time," they say. "Soon they'll have more interest in their community, more money, more responsibility, more something, and they will want to join." And to these associations I say, "Don't hold your breath." If younger generations aren't joining your association, there's a reason. It has absolutely nothing to do with their immaturity and everything to do with your association's inability to deliver value to them.

According to the *Generations and the Future of Association Participation* report, published by The William E. Smith Institute for Association Research, "There is a huge difference between Generation X and Baby Boomers with respect to the interest younger people show in being involved only by way of paying a fee—that is, in joining organizations that don't feature any tangible returns or real participation for the member."

The report concludes that while there are slightly fewer Generation Xers coming into their peak professional years as Baby Boomers begin to retire, they show a high willingness to join associations.

The net effect has the potential to be positive for the association community.

However, the report also concludes that Generation X "puts more demands on the organizations they support," expecting more information and involvement opportunities. Generation X is twice as unlikely as Baby Boomers to join an association offering a minimal return on investment.

The report advises that "associations will do well to treat membership issues proactively, developing strategies for increasing interest among Generation X and Y members."

Our society has observed considerable change in the past 60 years. As a result, each generation has been influenced by different life events and possesses different values. Rapidly changing technology, economic decline, and demographic shifts have challenged associations and many are reporting declining memberships. At least, there's been a movement away from membership associations as they have been known in the past. The table on the next page gives you a snapshot of generational characteristics and what they want from association membership.

Baby Boomers have been—and in most cases still are—associations' target market. But if you want your association to grow and sustain growth, your target market needs to shift to Generations X and Y, the New Recruits.

Knowing that the values of Generations X (1965–1981) and Y (1982–1995) tend to be focused on three primary objectives—the opportunity to lead, the opportunity to learn, and the opportunity to make a difference—is critical for focusing on membership outcomes. All members—regardless of age—need to feel like they belong. Your association doesn't see much turnover within the Baby Boomer membership because you are satisfying their need to belong. But what about the other generations? Do they feel like they belong in your association?

As a Generation Xer, I've been recruited by many associations wanting to increase their membership among young professionals. I was invited to give a presentation at an association

	Baby Boomers	Generation X	Generation Y
Born	1946–1964	1965–1981	1982–1995
Size	78 million	48 million	80 million
Nicknames	Me Generation, Love Generation, The Gray Ceiling	Slackers, MTV Generation	Millennials, Echo Boomers, Trophy Generation
Characteristics	Hard-working, loyal, confident, competitive	Anti-authority, self-reliant, family focused	Digital thinkers, feel entitled, needy
Why They Are the Way They Are	Grew up in a time of affluence. Reared to pursue the American Dream.	Children of workaholics and divorce, cable television. Reared to be self-sufficient.	Micro-managed by parents, technology, always rewarded for participation. Reared to be high achievers.
Communication Styles	Prefer detailed dialogue in-person or via phone. Appreciate meetings. Believe no news is good news.	Prefer clear, concise communication—not over-explaining, clichés, or corporate jargon. Prefer e-mail.	Prefer frequent feedback and problem solving via technology instead of phone calls or meetings.
Problems They Are Facing Right Now	Dwindling retirement funds, job dislocation, rising health care costs or inadequate health care coverage.	Debt, caring for young children and aging parents, balancing life and career, stuck in middle management.	Debt, unemployment, difficulty transitioning from college to career, negative stereotypes, being taken seriously.
Why They Join	Opportunities to lead and leave a legacy.	Opportunities to further their careers.	Opportunities to learn from others.
Volunteer Styles	Want to lead. Like to manage others. Like to hold meetings and discuss strategies.	Want autonomy. Hate being micromanaged or anything that wastes their time.	Want structure. Expect immediate feedback and increasing responsibility.
Flaws	Have a "been there done that" attitude, not always open to new ideas.	Have difficulty committing, tend to have a "wait-and-see" approach.	Have short attention spans and high demands and ask "what's in it for me?"
Turn-offs	People suggesting they try something new.	Chaos, distrust, loyalty that goes unrewarded.	Dismissing their ideas because of their lack of experience.

meeting. The meeting was held in my own backyard in Minneapolis, but I had never been to one of these meetings. I knew very little about the association itself, and I didn't know anyone in the room.

As the guest speaker, I was introduced to a few people during a brief lunch, then I gave a presentation about generational differences and shortly thereafter the meeting adjourned. On my way out, I was shocked when someone pulled me aside and asked me to join the association right then and there. He had a membership application in his hand. There was no way I was going to join that association that day! I didn't know any members and I had just met the association. I was sitting among strangers. How could I feel like I belonged? My most basic need had not yet been met. Perhaps I should have felt flattered but, instead, I felt awkward. I couldn't get out of that room fast enough.

People my age and younger are turned off by hard-pressure sales and we want the opportunity to warm up to a situation before we make a commitment. Jumping out of the bushes with a membership application in hand shortly after we meet isn't going to woo us over. That strategy is likely to backfire.

At one time I was recruited to serve on a board of directors. I was told I'd be given the opportunity to spearhead a priority initiative for the organization. It was a topic I was passionate about and an association I was invested in. I jumped at the opportunity to take on such a prominent role. Imagine my disappointment when the initiative was tabled at the first board meeting I attended. Over the next several meetings, the initiative continued to be postponed, and I found myself wondering what I was doing there. I was frustrated and disappointed, and my admiration for the association waned. Suddenly, I felt like I no longer belonged—or that I didn't want to belong.

Belonging means two things. It means that you have a secure relationship and it means that you have ownership in something. In many ways, belonging to an association is the equivalent of trusting in it. From a generational perspective, Baby Boomers trust more readily and are more accepting of lapses in trust behaviors than Generations X and Y.

It probably has something to do with how Generations X and Y were raised. Generation X were children of divorce, have never known job security, are all too familiar with telemarketing, and closely observed (via cable television and technology) many of the nation's leaders lying and failing to deliver on their promises. Likewise, Generation Y has had many of the same influences. In addition, they were young during the fall of entire corporations like Enron and the outbreaks of school shootings and terrorism.

To build trust with Generations X and Y, heed these tips:

- **Listen to their point of view.**
  Try to understand how things look from the perspective of Generations X and Y. What they want and expect from your association is different from what Boomers want and expect. This includes a frank examination of the flaws or weaknesses of your association. Invite young professionals to meet with your association leaders over lunch or coffee. Ask open-ended questions and set aside your assumptions. Empathize and let them know when you understand them; ask for examples when you don't.

    Remember, generational differences aren't a matter of right and wrong. What one generation prefers isn't better than what another generation prefers, but there are clearly differences in each generation's preferences. Not right. Not wrong. Just different.

Universally, people associate trust with being treated with respect. This means someone listened to you and took what you said into account even if that person didn't agree with you. Listening is the first step toward building a relationship of trust.

- **Create solutions.**

Make it your association's priority to generate new ideas and creative alternatives. Trust isn't built from trying to win personal victories. Some associations refuse to be solution-oriented. The leadership chooses to engage in a tug-of-war either among themselves or with the membership, fostering a competitive, territorial, and sometimes downright nasty environment.

If your membership is bleeding members, does it really make sense to argue over whether to continue using Robert's Rules of Order? Or whether to spend 80 percent of a staff person's time on lobbying instead of 50 percent? Internal arguments over everything from websites, mission statements, and board terms to who's buying lunch are counterproductive.

Keep in mind that your association is a business. Any conflict costs your association actual dollars in lost productivity and revenue. Resolve conflict by identifying each other's motives, goals, and agendas and clarify points of mutual agreement and interdependence. Together, come up with every possible solution.

- **Encourage feedback.**

To demonstrate listening, it is essential to have something to listen to. Thus, creating a space for people to contribute is essential. The space does not have to be lengthy; it can be enough to say in a meeting that for the next 10 minutes, the issue will be discussed by the group.

Some associations have had success hosting coffee chats for the purpose of initiating conversations between members and the board president or association CEO. A similar idea is "lunch for 12," a monthly lunch meeting when the president or CEO meets with 12 different members each month.

Other ideas include hosting online chats between members and association staff at specific times each week or month, hosting focus groups, or providing a means for members to submit their feedback via a suggestion box or dedicated voice mailbox. When members are able to express their ideas freely and build relationships with your staff, the levels of trust and the sense of belonging will increase. When members are able to express their ideas freely and build relationships with your staff, the levels of trust and the sense of belonging will increase.

An environment in which only your executives and board members have permission to share ideas and solve problems seriously hinders an association's potential for innovation, problem-solving, and relationship-building.

It's critical to have a means for responding to all this feedback, though. Make sure your association implements a way to let members know how you are following up on their suggestions. And by all means, if you say you're going to do something, do it. There's nothing worse than not following up on your promises.

- **Be inclusive.**

Remember that each generation has something of value to contribute to your association. It's amazing how many associations refuse the leadership of young professionals, claiming that they lack experience. Yet, what today's young professionals lack in experience they make up in other areas. They are better educated than most Boomers, more tech-savvy and entrepreneurial, globally-minded, and very creative.

More importantly, the Xs and Ys will outnumber the Boomers by 2015. Their perspectives should be represented at the decision-making table. Your association's leadership is only part of your association. And if your association's leaders are all over age 50, the voice of only one demographic is being represented.

Associations must move from being exclusive in regard to leadership to being inclusive and open to new ideas and skills for navigating the future. Purposely excluding people from any aspect of your association's operations is a sure-fire way to kill their sense of belonging and trust.

Generations X and Y need to feel a secure relationship and a sense of ownership in your association before they join. In contrast, most Baby Boomers will join an association because they feel it's the right thing to do and they work at the belonging piece of it after the fact. However, your association will struggle to recruit and retain younger members if they don't feel like they belong in your association. As soon as you understand the significance of that need, your association can begin to make progress towards meeting it. Building trust is done in steps and over time. It's not an immediate reaction, and neither is a sense of belonging.

Target Market Potential

Associations are struggling to engage the next generation of members either because they don't understand what they need or because they don't understand their potential. What I mean by potential is simply this: Younger generations hold all the power.

Whether you realize it or not, they have the potential to make or break your association.

The passage of the Baby Boomers will mark the end of an era, the end of the membership association as we know it. As this book is being written in 2011, 10,000 Baby Boomers are turning 65 every day. That trend will continue every day for the next 19 years.

Unfortunately, the recent dip in the economy put some people's minds at ease. Many believe the Boomers will postpone their retirements and our nation will continue to work and do business exactly as it always has done forever and ever. But retirements are not the problem. The lackadaisical attitude toward the largest shift in human capital in history is the problem.

Whether people are being overly optimistic or they're in downright denial, they are choosing to ignore the facts. By 2015, Baby Boomers will cede the majority of the workforce to Generation Y. Coupled with Generation X, that's 120 million people under age 50 who will be wielding power. For the first time since they came of age, the Baby Boomers won't be in power. Younger generations will hold the majority in the workforce population, the vote, and consumer spending. They will be relied on to move into positions of power and lead every industry.

Membership associations that refuse to implement change and interest younger members have a 10-year life-span—at most. A few associations have already gone by the wayside.

Patti Tanji serves on the executive committee for **Minnesota Business Women**. Once the state chapter of **Business and Professional Women**, the chapter evolved into a statewide association after BPW folded. "We're a statewide organization now because our national organization, BPW, is no longer a member-focused group. They had to close down as an association because BPW couldn't attract members like it used to," she explains. "BPW continues to exist as a nonprofit, but it's solely focused on advocacy, public policy, and grant work."

Even as a stand-alone association, MBW faces the same problem that BPW faced—attracting new members. Despite launching a robust website and new programming, Tanji notes MBW is an association run entirely by volunteers. She believes that membership model is the most threatened by shifts in society and demographics.

"We're still struggling. Five years from now will really be a telltale sign. I really think it's a sign of the times. The era of running these all-volunteer organizations is really coming to a close," she says. "People don't really need associations to build relationships anymore."

However, Tanji also notes that MBW casts a wide net for members, lacks a niche, competes with many other like-minded associations, and has not purposely targeted younger members. In other words, MBW (and BPW for that matter) has failed to meet the needs of younger generations, but it also has failed to recognize the potential of these generations.

Modern Woodmen of America, a fraternal benefits society steeped in tradition and serving more than 750,000 members in 2,400 chapters nationwide, took a century-old model and modernized it. Since 1883, Modern Woodmen has been a fraternal benefits society, offering life insurance, annuity, investments, banking products, and fraternal opportunities in communities. It is the third largest fraternal society in the nation, boasting 2,400 chapters.

Over the past few years, we've seen we've been attracting fewer members—especially fewer young families—because society is changing and getting busier," explains Jason Nickles, field development representative. The association's leadership boards weren't actively engaged or were becoming one-person shows."

Modern Woodmen became concerned that the same people were attending events, leading chapters, and doing the same things they had done for 20 years. Young people weren't being given an opportunity to lead. The organization took a serious look at chapter operations and made some changes. It wasn't an easy task. Most of the internal workings of Modern Woodmen had remained intact since its founding in 1883.

"We were looking at rewriting years and years of history. We were really concerned about how old members would react," Nickles recalls. The organization communicated continually from the beginning, talking to field representatives, hosting town hall meetings, and getting feedback from members over the course of several months.

At the Modern Woodmen convention, the membership voted unanimously in favor of the changes proposed. For starters, chapter terminology was updated. The association was still using the terminology from the early 1900s. The other shift was to focus membership on a new target market: young adults and students. Modern Woodmen updated the chapter boards and worked with leaders directly to help them recruit new people, encouraging outreach to young adults and student leaders.

Modern Woodmen introduced new tools to help young volunteers conduct board meetings. The organization requests that its chapter leaders set goals and determine which activities they want to host to support those goals, which are largely focused on community service. Modern Woodmen started to provide funding for chapter activities and board meetings to further demonstrate support for chapter operations and chapter leaders.

Modern Woodmen has received positive feedback and renewed energy in response to the changes it made. The organization is especially excited about infusing the participation of young people.

"Honoring your history is good. We still cherish our history and always will. But there comes a time when history prevents you from moving forward. You have to take a leap of faith and say it's time to change," Nickles says. "There's still a place for associations, but if they don't adapt to today's society, you will see some of them shrink. You have to bring relevant values to the organization. What was valuable yesterday isn't valuable today. "

The Loyalists

The Boomer generation, as the generations that came before it, is fiercely loyal to membership associations. Boomers tend to view membership associations as opportunities to build beneficial relationships, effect change, make a difference, and help others. They want a successful career and they want to make the world a better place, and membership associations are one place where they can do both. You probably have a pretty good handle on what this market wants. Nevertheless, here are a few strategies for keeping your most loyal customers.

The key to success lies in your association's ability to tap into each market's needs. With most of your Boomer membership holding executive-level and CEO roles, the ticket to keeping them engaged is to offer executive-level deliverables and executive-only communities.

A 2011 article "Attracting Executive-Level Members," written by Curtis Nunley, in ASAE's Membership Development e-newsletter reported that the **American Society of Civil Engineers** rolled out a response plan to engage more leaders of engineering firms. Their plan addressed the needs of executives, including:

- **Corporate visits.** The ASCE executive director, board president, and other association leaders visit with engineering leaders to remind them of the value ASCE brings to their organizations. During these visits, engineering leaders are engaged and, in some cases, join. At the least, these leaders have a greater understanding of the work ASCE does in support of their organizations, the profession, and individual engineers.

- **Industry awards.** ASCE awards expert individuals and decided to add a new awards category: Outstanding Projects and Leaders (OPAL), in which projects are also acknowledged. These projects are represented by firms and agencies, and the black-tie awards event brings recognition to firms and their leaders.

- **Industry Leaders Council (ILC).** The ILC serves as an advisory group for the board. It provides an opportunity for executives to interact on engineering issues and to interact with ASCE volunteer leaders.

- **ILC Tours.** ASCE started to arrange tours for members of the ILC to locations such as the *Truman* aircraft carrier and the World Trade Center redevelopment. The tours offer leaders a level of access to projects from other firms and agencies that they would not typically have. Discussions related to these project tours are engineering related, not business related, which is unique.

- **CEO panel.** At the ASCE Annual Meeting, industry leaders are invited to speak on a panel to discuss the business issues faced by engineers and, in particular, those leading engineering firms.

ASCE's efforts are paying off. Nunley writes that the association has seen significant growth in the group program, from 45 group members to 650. In many cases, ASCE has at least gained exposure with CEOs or agency directors, who now know much more about ASCE than they did before.

Menu Diversification

There's a strong case in favor of recruiting and retaining younger generations, but don't fold up your prosperous pizza-making business and start a spaghetti factory. Start thinking of your association as a buffet. Right now the tide is turning. It's 2011 and your most loyal customer base has started to shrink. You may not even notice anything happening yet, but it will. With each passing year, it will get a little smaller and 20 years from now, it won't even exist.

The question is: Will your association still exist? Younger generations have different needs and wants. Their appetite is different. Ignore them, and they will find somewhere else to eat. And I'm not talking about feeding a few goldfish. At 120 million people, Generations X and Y are the equivalent of a herd of elephants! They have the power to make or break your association.

Start thinking about all the needs within your membership and cater to them all. It's the only way to keep your association from going bankrupt.

5

Building Online Communities

"The basis of enchantment is not your Twitter account. The basis of enchantment is that you're likable and trustworthy."

Guy Kawasaki

Can you do the tango on Twitter?

Several years ago—maybe 12 years, which is the equivalent of 25 years when you're referring to technology)—I was consulting with an association that was contemplating the development of a new website. The leadership was worked up. "How will we ever keep our members? Our association was built on relationships! We'll lose members if we switch everything to the web!" Remember those days? Of course, we all know the ending to that story. Associations have managed to launch websites without losing members. In fact, in many instances technology ended up being the portal that drove increases in membership. Nevertheless, associations are still fearful of investing too much in technology. It's not just a website or just a blog anymore. We're starting to hear more and more about the evolution of online communities. (Oh, the horror! Whatever will become of our networking or our annual conference?)

After all, since their founding, associations have been largely focused on in-person deliverables. In-person meetings, workshops, conferences, golf tournaments, meals, handshakes, winks, and smiles have been at the core of every association's existence. It's how they've delivered value and customer service. What most associations fail to realize is that technology has the same capability.

Have you ever visited a website expecting something really great, only to come across a site that was outdated, text-heavy, and the opposite of charming in every way? When that happens, our perception of the association is altered and we leave the site immediately. It's the equivalent of having bad table manners or looking like you slept in your suit the night before a big meeting.

Which brings me back to my question: Can you do the tango on Twitter? The answer is yes, you can! Technology gives you a whole suite of tools and capabilities for communicating to members through audio, video, chats, blogs, and all types of media. Technology is something to embrace as yet another way to deliver value and customer service. When used to its fullest capacity, technology is a robust brand-building, community-building tool and influential user interface.

Technology can never replace an in-person experience, but that's not to dismiss technology as an insufficient tool. Quite the opposite! Remember this: What engages people online isn't much different than what connects them in person. It's entirely possible to communicate an experience, a brand, a smile, and a polite handshake through technology. It may not be the same or a better experience than the in-person experience, but think about how you're using technology to engage, captivate—even tango—with your audience.

Community-Building Online

You have generations coming to the table who have been raised on technology and expect the opportunity to access your association's offerings through technology. So, if what engages us online is similar to what connects us in person, what is your technology saying about your association? Is it well dressed? Friendly? Professional? An online community is really just an extension of your association.

You think nothing of inviting your members to fly to Puerto Rico or some other destination for your annual conference. When your members arrive, you have worked on every aspect to make sure the event experience is reflective of your association's brand: ample signage, courteous greeters at the registration desk, great food, renowned speakers, everything to the last detail. Your online community planning and design should be no different. It's the compilation of great tools and resources used to create a virtual meeting with your members.

For now, you may be referring to it as your website, but a website is really just an ad for your association, an "about us" page. Your association must transform its website into an online community—a place where information is actively shared, people interact, and they frequently visit your site to access valuable information and resources. Many associations have successfully created online communities, some of which will be mentioned later in this chapter. They've used technology to flip their fortunes and build their influence.

Here are a few tips for creating a remarkable online community of your own.

- **Appoint a Leader.**
  Your association will fail miserably at implementing each of the following tips if it doesn't first appoint someone to

oversee your community-building efforts. You can't build a great city without a mayor. You can't build a beautiful building without a construction manager. And you can't build an online community without someone directing the project and keeping it updated every day. Appoint at least one person on your staff or within your volunteer corps to assume the very important role of community manager.

An online community is no small undertaking. Ensure you have the capacity within your organization to deploy, market, and maintain the online community. Also be sure there is support from leadership to integrate the online community throughout all areas of your association.

- **Give Up Control.**
Equally as important as appointing a leader is the willingness to relinquish control. Just as you can't control what people say about you behind your back, you can't control the conversation online either. Sometimes people will sing your praises. Sometimes they won't. Perhaps the people who are criticizing you have a point. Maybe it's your fault. Maybe it's not and you want to set the story straight. Either way, you have an opportunity to respond to your members and fix problems, which is a win-win situation. But you must be willing to give up control.

- **Find an Expert.**
I'm speaking from experience. I tried to launch an online community for my business a few years ago. It fell flat and I was out a huge chunk of change because I hired the wrong vendor. Do your homework. Research, interview, and ask for referrals. Make sure your selected vendor has experience and resources with social media and has an understanding of the unique needs of associations. For the best results, choose

a creative vendor that produces engaging yet simple user-interface designs.

- **Determine Your Mission.**

  Before implementing an online community, it's important to understand how the tools will benefit the organization's mission. Based on your analysis of how an online community could support your mission and what features your members would find valuable, you should be able to clearly identify what features you need. Many Web 2.0 features are available. Don't choose tools based on novelty or industry buzz. Choose tools that will help your association achieve its purpose.

- **Tell Your Story.**

  On any given day, there are hundreds of stories your association could tell. There are stories about your members, the latest bill on Capitol Hill that you're lobbying against, your industry or region, and the latest member roundtable or convention. Online communities provide platforms for telling these stories and support the efforts of your association through Twitter feeds, Facebook, webinars, and blogs. Actively participate in the conversation. Tell your association's story so members and nonmembers alike can build relationships with your association, embrace its mission, and spread the word.

- **Be Timely.**

  When's the last time your website was updated? Does the content change? Information on the main pages of the site that has not been updated in three years speaks volumes about an association. A browser sees an outdated site and jumps to negative conclusions about that association's operations, customer service, and communications practices. Driving traffic to your site is important but not sustainable if the information you provide is irrelevant. Relevance is critical.

- **Engage Your Audience.**

While recently working on a project for an association, I interviewed several of its members. Every interview was the same. The member started out chatting up all the association's offerings. The association did this and did that. Then I'd ask about value and it was all downhill from there.

Some associations really excel at serving their members—lobbying, providing information, hosting events, publishing newsletters, and so on. But few associations really excel at delivering value—actually making a member's job easier or life better. When people are engaged, they are moved by their membership. They believe membership makes a substantial difference for them and they actively promote your association to others.

Find ways to use your online community to deliver more value to your members or at least to engage them in sharing their ideas about how to improve the membership experience.

For example:

- Poll your members to find out which hot topics they'd like to discuss, and then host regularly scheduled weekly or monthly chats about those topics;

- Host live chats with thought-leaders, authors, speakers and other experts, allowing your members to post questions and "chat" with them.

- Encourage the formation of member-driven niche discussion groups and organize informal local member meet-ups.
- Give members the opportunity to collaborate on or bid on projects.

- **Use Your Influence.**
Technology has given your association the power to influence more decisions, dialogue, and change. Encourage your members to lobby on your behalf via social networks, educate your members about various legislation, start discussions on topics of interest, launch competitions, share ideas, ask for feedback. Whatever you do, take the lead. Your members want to be part of something really great, something really influential. No one wants to follow a follower. They want to follow a leader.

- **Keep Working on It.**
Building an online community is no different than building an effective educational program or meeting; you must analyze the situation, develop a strategy, design your product, develop it, reflect on it, and keep working on it. The notion that you will be able to simply write pages of content and put it out there is too simplistic.

For starters, create an implementation plan. It is not always practical to launch a full-featured online community all at once. Consider rolling out features in phases, giving your association (and your members) a chance to get comfortable with the most important features first.

Next, design a marketing strategy. The online community should not be its own island separate from the rest of your association activities and communications. Actively promote the benefits of the online community through email blasts, events, and publications.

Be sure to measure your success. Whether you measure log-ins, downloads, ad placement, or the number of mentions via social media, track your members' use of the online community. This information can help you gauge how successful your community is and be responsive to community interests and needs.

An online community is a work in progress. Whatever you do, don't launch it and leave it.

- **Just Do It.**

To borrow from the famous sneaker company's tagline, just do it. Your association needs to get its community launched sooner than later. Technology is rapidly changing and your members' expectations are also changing. If you don't build a community for them, it's possible your competition or your members will do it themselves. Then why would your members need you?

Your association must take the lead. That's the difference between successful and unsuccessful associations. Successful associations jump in the pool and unsuccessful associations just talk about jumping in the pool but never actually do it.

The fact is, technology is here to stay. Stop fearing it and start embracing it. More technology has been developed in the last five years than in the previous 50 years. We're all on a merry-go-round of innovation, driving us to adopt new technology, stay competitive, share more information, and create more, more, more. Either your association keeps up with the change or it falls woefully behind.

What engages us online isn't that much different than what engages us in person. Whether they are searching your site or sitting in the audience at an event, your members are seeking answers to their problems. If your association is there for them, regardless of where they look first, you will interest them. And if you focus on making their on-line experience as impressive and service-oriented as their in-person experiences with your association, you will engage them.

Mission Possible

Technology may be the exact tool your association needs to further its membership mission. Consider these examples.

American Institute of Certified Public Accountants (AICPA)

The Mission: Target college and high school students and encourage them to major in accounting.

A great example of an online community is "Start Here. Go Places." Concerned about the future of the industry's talent pipeline, AICPA launched the site (www.StartHereGoPlaces. com) to spearhead a comprehensive student recruitment effort. The site has been successful in meeting its mission. Launched in 2001, the site has been growing interest in the accounting industry among the target population. AICPA launched an updated version of the site in 2010 and within a year, more than 27,000 students had created profiles on the site.

Start Here Go Places includes many features targeted toward students, such as the opportunity to create a custom profile; access interesting career information; learn about internships, scholarships, and colleges; network with other students; play games; view video profiles; and read compelling stories of CPAs in fascinating work environments. What really started as an online campaign successfully morphed into an online community. Now,

AICPA is taking the community off-line, as well. In addition to the site, AICPA introduced a print magazine for students, an e-zine, and a 10-part workshop called Money Means Business as well as other programming.

To further the association's mission, AICPA introduced a special section on the website for educators. The educator section houses resources for teachers to use in high school and college classrooms, such as business simulations and online workshops.

Metropolitan Milwaukee Area Chamber of Commerce (MMAC)

The Mission: Position the Milwaukee region as a destination for world-class talent.

When MMAC became concerned about the brain drain in Milwaukee, they appointed a group of young leaders charged with helping the Chamber recruit and retain young professionals. Interest in the cause was so great, that a new community was born. Fuel Milwaukee has success-fully met its mission, working closely with employers and talent to implement its regional talent strategy to improve Milwaukee's image, increase community engagement, and grow more contemporary workplaces.

Today, Fuel Milwaukee is composed of 6,000 members living and working in the Milwaukee region. The vast majority of Fuel's members (88 percent) are between the ages of 21 and 40. Fuel boasts a strong online presence. As the economic development initiative has grown, new technology continues to be implemented. Now, in addition to attending VIP-style networking events and community service projects, Fuel members can use their online community to peruse volunteer opportunities, register for events, participate in surveys, view event photos, join affinity groups, search for jobs, apply for awards, and access a cadre of resources to support their recruitment and retention efforts.

Snow and Ice Management Association (SIMA)

The Mission: Connect the professional snow and ice management industry.

In 2010, SIMA launched a social community and content hub for its industry called GoPlow.com. The site features valuable information about sales and marketing, finance and business operations, ice management equipment, and techniques in addition to a blog, magazine articles, and the opportunity to network with industry groups.

National Association of Manufacturers (NAM)

The Mission: Provide places online where people who are passionate about manufacturing can go to learn, share, and engage in social networking.

In the examples listed above, the associations created communities as stand-alone websites. The sites all feature links to their parent associations, but their site addresses, logos, and brands are not directly related to their parent associations. That's one approach. NAM has taken a different approach and houses all its Web 2.0 strategies in house. The association makes a point of stating on its site that it "operates numerous social media sites and online communities" for the purpose of creating and sharing industry news.

NAM promotes itself as being the provider of social media for manufacturers and promotes the following suite of offerings:

• Shopfloor, the leading issue advocacy blog for manufacturers since 2004;

- Facebook for Manufacturers, the leading tool for manufacturing advocates to connect and organize grassroots events;

- Twitter for Manufacturers, the leading social media channel for breaking manufacturing policy issue information;

- NAM's YouTube Channel, providing videos on a variety of manufacturing advocacy topics such as policy issues, election news, TV appearances, and a popular "Cool Stuff Being Made" series;

- LinkedIn for Manufacturers, a private group to provide a forum for leaders in the manufacturing and small business community to connect and share insight and experiences; and

- Additional participation on the following sites: SlideShare, Scribd, Foursquare, Yelp, Digg, Delicious ,and Google Places.

No Chapters, Only Communities

There isn't one recipe your association has to follow to effectively launch an online community. Unlike most associations, the **Indie Beauty Network** doesn't host an annual conference. In fact, IBN rarely hosts an in-person meeting. Here's the story of how IBN made their mission possible and built a successful membership model using nothing but technology.

Indie Beauty Network

The Indie Beauty Network helps independent (indie) business owners and manufacturers specializing in the beauty industry earn a fair profit and grow their companies.

Since its founding in 2000, IBN has grown to encompass 868 members in seven countries.

IBN's founder, Donna Marie Coles Johnson, credits technology for the association's success. As the former owner of a cosmetics company herself, Johnson knew the small business beauty market was underserved. "The other beauty trade organizations were all helping Revlon and the large cosmetic companies. When it comes to small business, their customers are different, their needs are different, and their pocketbook is different," she says.

So Johnson set out to create a trade organization that was affordable and delivered value to the independent beauty business. From the start, IBN did things differently. They used technology to provide trade forums, webinars, and networking. The goal was to build a trade organization that small businesses could afford to join. IBN may be organized as an online community, but it is still a trade organization. "We go to Capitol Hill, we meet with legislators and staffers for Congress, and we really work hard to change policies affecting our audience," Johnson says.

Johnson noted that IBN has successfully defeated legislation that would hurt the industry's small business owners and put them out of business. "I'm very proud of our track record as far as that's concerned," she says.

Additionally, technology has helped with nearly every aspect of running the association. It has helped IBN be more productive and efficient and to maintain a virtual work environment to keep costs down. Technology also has helped with IBN's marketing efforts and generated media attention. Furthermore, IBN has hosted numerous webinars, giving members access to the information, tips, ideas, and blueprints they need to be successful.

"Technology is making it possible to deliver so much more to my members that I can't imagine why other associations aren't also using it," Johnson says. IBN has been able to give great value to its members and build a healthy, interactive online community. While other associations started out doing everything in-person and moved slowly toward technology, IBN is doing just the opposite.

"We do have some face-to-face events in communities. Whenever I travel, I invite the members in that area out," Johnson says. "And we do meet online all the time. Those relationships can be just as intimate as face-to-face contact. Those sorts of relationships don't take the place of physical interaction, but they certainly do facilitate small business interaction and that's my goal."

Another example of an online community is **Women at the Top** (WATT). Founder Regina Barr explains that when she started WATT she knew she wanted to avoid using a chapter model for membership. Barr had her reasons for developing WATT as a virtual community of members. First and foremost, she wanted to avoid conflict.

"In my experience with chapters, members really run the chapters and they do it as a hierarchy. When it comes to engaging younger generations, that's not the structure they want. They don't want hierarchy or the same old model of coming to a program, watching a speaker present, and then leaving," she explains. "Plus, I wanted to give members the opportunity to network with one another and learn valuable information without the constraints of also having to lead the chapter."

Barr also had concerns that the economics of running an association wouldn't appeal to her members. The target member is a corporate woman, and the down economy has forced women to do more with less whether at work or at home. Since most chapters are based in large cities, members might spend 45 minutes or more driving to and from an event, often have to pay for parking, and spend two to three hours out of the office. The option for hosting an evening meeting was also out of the question because her members want to spend time with family then.

"I did research and I knew there was a need out there, but it had to be presented in a different way. That's why I knew WATT had to have a different model," Barr says. WATT provides its members, who are in senior-level roles or aspire to be, with access to exclusive and relevant information, high-level skills seminars, virtual conferences, author interviews, executive coaching and group coaching sessions, small group discussions referred to as virtual coffees, and other resources critical to their success.

WATT started as a free membership association. Barr used a sales funnel model to move people from free memberships to paying membership. "From a strictly business perspective, you need to have a model to filter people into the association. I launched WATT and hosted a huge virtual conference and didn't charge anything for it. That was my investment into WATT. I did it for visibility," she says. "If you look at a sales funnel, you should first get people signed up for access to information—your blog, monthly e-newsletter, or something that gives them value. You have to gain their trust, give them access, and then begin to upsell and convert people to membership. But first you need to build a relationship."

Community Redefined

In addition to founding WATT, Barr has served in leadership roles in several associations. She says she believes there is a place and a need for associations, but only if they are willing to change.

"I think there's going to have to be a sea change. The associations that can reinvent themselves and figure out how to take advantage of what's important to this up-and-coming generation are going to be vibrant and successful. For those that aren't willing to change and end up closing, then maybe it's for the better. Maybe it was time for them to go away."

Throughout history, community has been defined as a social group of any size whose members reside in a specific locality, share government, and often have a common culture and history. That definition has changed in recent years, partly because of demographic shifts and economic dips but largely because of technology. Technology has given us access to the world and the opportunity to network with anyone, anywhere, anytime.

In the past, communities were tight-knit and centered on the family and primary groups (coworkers, relatives, neighbors, close friends). Our interactions tended to be horizontal; that is, they took the form of personal, face-to-face encounters. In today's world, community may mean just a group of people with similar interests. We have more contact with people outside our primary group and we use a variety of mediums to communicate with them.

But one thing hasn't changed. Communities are still focused on relationships. Regardless of who you are, where you live, or what your age is, you need to be in a relationship with other people to survive. Likewise, your association must have a relationship with your members to survive. You can't stop communicating with them—or with anyone for that matter—and expect to have a good relationship. Be likeable, be trustworthy, and be present in the lives of your members and they will always want to engage with you.

6

Redefining Membership

"Sometimes by losing a battle you find a
new way to win the war."
Donald Trump

As I write this book, my daughter is planning to start her own ice
cream business. She's hoping to corner the market, stealing sales
away from the drive-by ice cream truck by offering a kid-friendly
sales concept. (She thinks adults in trucks shouldn't be selling
ice cream to children.) She's planning to decorate a creative,
portable ice cream cooler containing unique ice cream treats—
taste-tested by her, of course—that she can sell at neighborhood
ballparks on hot summer days.

I'm guessing that her new business will give her a fine lesson in
supply and demand. Will she sell more Bubble Yum Bomb Pops
or King Kong Bars? Will the temperature affect her sales? Will
she be able to sell ice cream on rainy days or only sunny days?
Will her sales vary by neighborhood?

I already know the answers to a couple of these questions. I did
a little research on ice cream sales and learned that fewer people
want to eat ice cream on cool or rainy days. That seems obvious,
right? Well, when it comes to business and trying to make sales,

sometimes the obvious just isn't obvious. Maybe that's why a lot of associations are standing in the pouring rain, still trying to sell ice cream to people who don't want to buy it.

As explained in the first chapter, three key shifts in our society have caused a decline in membership: economic recession, demographic shifts, and rapidly changing technology. While the economy is likely to rebound sooner or later, the other two influences are here to stay. We can't bring an end to technology or stop people from aging. These shifts are beyond our control— just like rainy days.

As a result of these shifts, the value of and demand for membership is declining. It comes down to pure economics: Value is minimized, demand declines as fewer people pay for memberships, then your association suffers losses in revenue until it shuts down or goes bankrupt.

Your association has two choices now: Make changes to increase the demand for membership, or stay the same and risk losing your members and eventually the entire association. It's the choice between survival and extinction. If you choose the path of survival, your association must first increase the value of membership. The past five chapters have addressed this topic in detail.

Next, you must assess your operations—those ongoing activities involved in running your association for the purpose of producing value for your members. Your operations can be boiled down to one key concept: the way in which your association generates income.

While your association probably receives income from a variety of revenue streams, the focus is membership revenue. If your organization is a membership association and the demand for memberships is declining, how do you get people to maintain their memberships and keep paying dues?

Membership Models

For hundreds of years association memberships have been cut from the same cloth. With few exceptions, people paid dues once a year for access to a full year's worth of membership. Today, membership associations are introducing a variety of operational models and revenue streams. Innovation is a must.

Five membership models have emerged: customized, electronic, international, multitier, and open. These models hold the most promise for associations to generate new revenue streams and grow membership.

The chart below provides a snapshot of the five models. Additional information about each model follows.

Emerging Membership Models

	Synopsis	The Pros	The Cons
Customized	Members' custom-build their membership packages to suit their interests and needs.	Members analyze how they want to use their membership, which leads to higher engagement.	Associations must conduct substantial membership research and allow time to transition all current members.
Electronic	Membership is restricted to web-based resources and programming.	New streams of revenue are added without incurring expenses (e.g., mailing and printing).	Memberships provide limited access so they cost less and therefore generate less revenue.
International	Membership is accessible to people worldwide.	Membership expands into new markets and regions; supports globalization efforts.	Programming and benefits may need to be developed; engagement more difficult.
Multitier	Menu of membership options based on interests, professional designation, budget.	Members like being able to choose which options best suit their needs.	Requires the ability to manage multiple benefits for multiple audiences.
Open	Membership does not require the payment of dues.	Leads to substantial membership growth.	People perceive there's no value because there's no cost to join.

Customized Membership

In the past 20 years or so, there has been a move away from conformity toward customization. It's now possible to customize everything from your jeans to your laptop, your stamps, music (iPod), and your M&Ms. Why not memberships, too? Every association has members who are highly engaged, attending every event and actively serving on committees. Every association also has members who are unengaged. They pay dues and might take advantage of a couple member benefits in a given year. Research shows the most unengaged members are the most at risk of leaving the association.

Customized memberships are one way associations can get their members more involved. The **Whitney Museum of American Art** in New York City created the Curate Your Own Membership program that allows members to select a membership with core benefits at a base price and then add on additional benefits. The customized membership program is the result of extensive research to clearly identify the types of benefits that members wanted.

Likewise, members of the **Corporate Executive Board**, an association of 5,200 of the world's leading corporations, can enhance their memberships by adding custom services for additional fees, including a series of four interactive webcasts, quarterly manager training, customized survey modules and an in-person executive workshop.

The customized membership model offered by **Stan Hywet Hall & Gardens**, a National Historic Landmark in Akron, Ohio, offers additional perks for free. Members can sign up for Joe's Club, a members-only perk, which admits the family dog(s) for free on Woof Walk Sundays, or a Kids Club featuring members-only access to several social and educational programs designed just for kids. Furthermore, when members share their reasons for joining, be it the love of gardening, connection with local history, the grounds for walking, or participating in special events, they receive a customized e-mail newsletter specific to their personal interests.

Customized membership are just beginning to evolve, but it's likely there will be more of them in the near future, as society continues its love affair with customization.

Electronic Membership

I remember sitting in a web class in 2000 when the instructor told us that within 10 years our cell phones would be computers. Your computer will be the size of your hand, he said. The room erupted into gasps of disbelief and giggles at the absolute insanity of the idea.

Yet, here we are riding a wave of technology that updates every 18 months or less. Rapidly changing technology has given us the capacity to network and do business with people all over the world. From Facebook to Skype to GoToMeeting, we can meet with anyone, anywhere at the click of a mouse. Not surprising, Generation Y is the first generation to spend more time online than watching television.

Also not surprising is the recent explosion of e-memberships, sometimes referred to as digital memberships. Associations everywhere are beginning to realize that membership doesn't have to be confined by geography or in-person meetings.

Optimist International (OI) launched eOptimist, an online community, in an attempt to reach younger members. Free members receive an e-newsletter, while members who pay $35 per year have additional access to webinars and audio interviews as well as opportunities to contribute to the eOptimist website and blog. Within a matter of months, OI had attracted approximately 1,600 members, a third of whom paid the $35 membership fee.

The **Mathematical Association of America** launched an all-electronic membership to include online access to all three MAA journals. All other membership benefits remain the same. E-membership dues cost the same as a basic membership, which includes a subscription to one print publication. In comparison, the e-membership provides online access to all three journals for the price of one print journal. This option not only provides an additional membership option, it also saves on MAA's printing costs and reduces environmental waste.

While some associations choose to charge nominal dues for electronic membership, others choose not to charge dues. The **American Dental Assistants Association** (ADAA) provides an e-membership to dental assistants worldwide for free. The membership provides online access to the association's journal, one free hour of online continuing education, e-newsletters, discussion boards, e-retail discounts, and continuing education discounts.

Whether or not your association makes its e-memberships dues-based, there's no question that e-memberships are a good alternative for growing membership. E-memberships allow you to easily deliver services to an international audience and to do so at a reduced cost and in an eco-friendly, paperless option.

International Membership

Many associations claim to be global organizations because they offer memberships to people residing in other countries. However, when evaluating whether or not to add international memberships to your roster, it is best to consider what services will be provided to international members, what increased costs (if any) are involved in serving this new membership class, and what benefits are included.

Some organizations treat international memberships similar to virtual or e-memberships, where the benefits include members-only access to website content, e-newsletters, and e-learning options but do not include face-to-face learning programs or print materials that are costly to mail internationally and frequently don't arrive to their intended recipients. For example, the **Institute of Electrical and Electronics Engineers** (IEEE) recently made the decision to give international members access to an e-membership option. The only change in member benefits is that publications are delivered electronically and the membership is offered at an affordable rate of just $50.

Other associations develop benefits unique to international members, such as international programming and content. **ARMA International** (Association of Records Managers and Administrators) has approximately 10,000 members in more than 30 countries. ARMA is home to an International Relations Committee (IRC) that represents the interests of the international members. ARMA has focused on the growth of this membership category, hosting an international conference and an International Day program dedicated to issues specific to records and information management professionals outside North America. In addition, ARMA provides several online courses, downloadable resources for international members, and a journal featuring articles about industry trends and how they are affecting the management of records and information around the world.

The **National Association of Home Builders** (NAHB) also touts international membership as a vital part of its members-only network and the association's mission to stay on the cutting edge of the housing industry's globalization. NAHB international members receive special rates on the International Builder's Show, education seminars, products, and other amenities that combine information sharing with networking opportunities. NAHB's International Department compiles resources and organizes events especially for its international audience and U.S. members interested in working globally.

Multitier Membership

Most associations have one level of membership providing all members identical benefits, whether the membership is offered to individuals or organizations. However, there are always members who want to buy the Cadillac of your association's membership offerings. They likely are your most active members. In contrast, you will always have members who want to buy the most basic membership, and there are members who fall between these two extremes as well.

A Multitier membership model offers several levels of membership and members pay according to the benefits offered within each tier. This model is sometimes referred to as "a la carte" membership. For example, an association might add a membership category that includes books as part of the membership. As soon as the association publishes a new book it is sent out to the higher dues paying "book members."

A great example of multitier membership is the model created by the **Association for Supervision and Curriculum Development** (ASCD), which provides five different membership options:

- Express Membership $29: online only services

- Basic Membership $49: online services plus subscriptions to the monthly periodical and newsletter

- Comprehensive Membership $89: basic benefits plus five association books shipped as they are published

- Premium Membership $219: all of the above plus an additional newsletter, four additional books and a $100 professional development voucher
- Institutional Membership $899: a package that includes one Premium membership and 10 Basic memberships.

SAE International (formerly the Society of Automotive Engineers) uses a similar approach. The association offers three different levels of membership and goes the extra mile to provide a Membership e-Valuator Tool to help members decide quickly and easily which level of membership is right for them.

The **American Occupational Therapy Association** (AOTA) provides 10 membership options categorized by occupation and ranging from occupational therapist to student and new practitioner, to post-professional doctorate and organizational associate. Membership benefits specifically address the members' interests and needs according to their current career paths.

Open Membership

Perhaps the most controversial membership model evolving right now is the open membership, also known as a free membership. Here are the most popular reasons that associations give for looking to innovate their membership models with "no-dues" structures:

- **Increase Membership**
  Associations see an opportunity to bring more people, especially young people, into their communities by offering engagement opportunities that don't require a financial commitment up front.

- **Develop Thought Leadership**

  Associations see an opportunity to produce insightful, original, and helpful ideas and move their mission further than they can with structured membership programs.

- **Offer Value**

  Associations with decreasing membership are often tired of fighting to explain the value of a membership come renewal time. Eliminating dues for most members and allowing members to pay for only the programs and services that they find valuable can boost an association's value proposition by making the value it provides fit each member's unique situation.

The question of whether to collect dues is not the same for all associations. Missions, membership, and values differ from one association to the next. The art of pricing is specific to individual markets, offerings, and value propositions.

From the omission of dues to their reliance on technology and crowd sourcing, **Senior Planners Industry Network** (SPIN) flipped the traditional association model upside down. Here's how this association created its own membership model for success.

Senior Planners Industry Network

SPIN is a network of 2,300 top-level meeting and event planners throughout the world, all with at least 10 years of experience. Started in 2008, the association grew quickly, averaging 75 new members per month.

Shawna Suckow, founder of the association, started the association when she realized there weren't any associations targeting senior-level meeting planners. Also, she purposely wanted to create something substantially different than any other association. "I believe that today's association model is outdated. It's evident in the lagging membership numbers as well as in the imbalance between vendors and buyers. In our industry—the meeting industry—many of the major associations have memberships that are 70 percent vendors, which frustrates everyone. Events lose their focus; vendors don't see the ROI when most of the crowd is their competition; and buyers don't keep coming each month when their peers make up such a small percentage of the group," Suckow explains. "I also believe that associations charge way too much just for the privilege of membership without any real, tangible value. Then to be charged for each monthly meeting on top of that is too much to ask."

SPIN offers members access to a private on-line forum full of resources and webinars for educational purposes. Shortly after its founding, SPIN launched live networking and educational events held at locations throughout the United States.

"The membership determines what they want to discuss at our live events and which cities we visit. We try to 'crowd source' everything, meaning we constantly ask the membership what they want, and then we deliver it," Suckow says.

SPIN is free to join, but members must meet two strict criteria: Members must be planners with a minimum of 10 years experience. Vendors are prohibited from membership. This keeps the network focused strictly on planner needs and avoids the need to cater to other interests in educational programming. Vendor participation is permitted in the form of sponsorships at SPIN's live events called Think Tanks, but participation is limited to only six companies per event.

"We believe keeping the focus on the planner is what has made us so successful in such a short time. It's unique in our industry to be planner-centric, especially focused on senior-level planners. I believe these niche networks are the association model of the future," Suckow says. "Our association model is inadvertently putting pressure on the huge associations to adapt or continue to see their memberships decrease," Suckow says. "The old association model is dying and I don't believe it can be revived, even when the economy recovers. I talk to buyers and vendors all the time, and both sides complain to me regularly about the major associations in our industry.

Suckow believes the intense focus on delivering value to a very specific niche and not trying to be everything to everyone has resulted in a more meaningful, ROI-driven association for SPIN's members. SPIN is now traveling to multiple cities and selling out their sponsorships. Not surprising, Suckow has become an advocate for associations to experiment with new, innovative membership models.

"I believe in survival of the fittest. If you keep doing what you've always done, you're going to continue to bleed memberships and lose sponsorships," she says. "Associations have to adapt and make difficult choices to regain the support of lost membership and reinvigorate their groups."

More Models

In addition to the five models listed above, the following models also provide a means for helping associations flip their fortunes.

Lifetime Membership

Give members the opportunity to pay for a lifetime membership, which means the member will never have to pay dues again. For example, the **National Sheriff's Association**'s Paid-Up-For-Life Program is a one-time fee based on the member's age and the size of the county the sheriff represents. NSA's Paid-For-Life

Members receive numerous benefits, including $10,000.00 accidental death and dismemberment Insurance, 30 percent off NSA's Annual Conference registration, and discounts on national and regional trainings.

Career Transition Membership

These memberships allow professionals to maintain their memberships during a time of transition, whether that's retirement, job loss, or transitioning from college to career. When **Minnesota Women in Marketing and Communications** noticed it was losing a certain percentage of members each year to maternity leave and child care sabbaticals, the association introduced a Career-On-Hold membership. The membership costs less than a full membership but delivers many of the same benefits. In return for the discount, MWMC asks its Career-On-Hold Members to volunteer a number of hours per year to the chapter. This helps members keep their networks and skills intact while taking a leave of absence to care for children and also sustains membership and revenues for MWMC.

Student Membership

Student memberships pose a tremendous opportunity for growth, especially considering Generation Y is the largest generation in American history. There are 80 million high school and college students just waiting for an association to engage them. A number of ways to recruit students exist, including forming student chapters, creating alliances with local universities or colleges, offering mentoring programs, providing discounted memberships, or hosting job fairs and other events geared toward students.

Associations are now challenged to think of student chapter development more as a community where students go for resources or support, and the best resource for that community is the students themselves. The **National Kitchen and Bath Association** (NKBA) started recruiting students as early as 2005 as a way to resolve an industry-wide worker shortage. Presently, NKBA is home to 33 student chapters and supports accredited design programs at more than 50 colleges and universities.

The NKBA annual student membership costs $15 and provides access to the only industry-specific listing of internships and full-time positions, discounted professional development courses, a resource library, several levels of certification in kitchen and bath design, and free admission to the Kitchen/Bath Industry Show & Conference. NKBA also hosts an annual student design competition and offers exclusive scholarship opportunities to NKBA members.

Young Professional Membership

In the early 2000s, associations targeted toward young professionals started popping up everywhere. Virtually overnight there were 90 "YP" groups nationwide. Most were stand-alone associations not affiliated with existing associations.

As an association executive, you may be familiar with such an organization—**Young Association Professionals** (YAP), an online network of 1,267 association professionals. The group also hosts online and live events. One of most successful YP groups launched in 2003, the **Boston Young Professionals Association** (BYPA), is still going strong. With more than 12,000 members, BYPA hosts 150 unique events ranging from black-tie balls to community service projects. BYPA remains the only networking organization for young professionals in Boston.

As soon as established associations started realizing the power of young professional groups—and the potential risk of losing their youngest members—they introduced young professional membership categories themselves.

For example, the **Institute of Management Accountants** (IMA) offers young professionals, which IMA has specified as ages 32 and younger, a unique membership at a 33 percent savings from professional member dues. This special membership level focuses on responding to the needs of young professionals, including Certified Management Accountant (CMA) certification, continuing education courses, and access to LinkUp IMA—a members-only online network including opportunities to connect job-seeking members with employers.

Monthly Automatic Payment Membership

If you think about it, our society has moved to a month-by-month financial focus. Your cell phone, internet, car payment, and service contracts are paid monthly. Netflix has built an empire on monthly subscriptions to the on-demand internet streaming movie service for as low as $8 per month. It's unlikely we would purchase any of these products if we were required to pay for them a year in advance. We are also more likely to continue the services when the payments are automatically debited from our credit card or bank account.

Most business, trade, social, and civic membership associations do not offer the opportunity to pay dues monthly. A member is typically required to pay a full year's dues up front. Associations also spend a considerable amount of resources sending out annual dues notices and follow-up reminders to try to get members to renew their dues on time or renew them at all. The monthly membership model helps associations sustain their revenue streams and simplify their retention efforts.

The **Association for Medical Imaging Management** (AHRA) uses a monthly membership option, debiting the dues monthly until a member decides to cancel. AHRA positions the option as an option that's easier for members to manage and budget for in comparison to paying dues in "one lump sum."

Trial Membership

There is a long history of using free trial offers in membership marketing. In essence, a free trial offer substitutes providing member services for marketing efforts. It's an attempt to have the product sell itself. Tony Rossell, senior vice president of Marketing General, authored a blog in March 2010 about the types of trial memberships and conversion rates. A summary of his data follows.

- **Opt-in Trial**

  This method features an initial promotion to prospects and asks them to accept a membership trial. Upon acceptance, the respondent receives membership for a specified period of time and additional promotions requesting that he or she join. Depending on the quality of the list, the initial response can be between three and five percent. The final conversion to paid membership can be about 30 percent.

- **Forced Free Trial**

  This method provides a free trial to a qualified audience that did not specifically ask for the trial. It may be a list that you have compiled or that is supplied to you by current members or another source. Services are provided to these prospective members for a period of time and then prospects are asked to convert to a paid status. The final conversion rate from a well qualified list can be about 10 percent.

- **No-Obligation Trial**

  When a prospect agrees to this trial, he or she also agrees to allow the organization to invoice them for the membership. The respondent has the choice to pay an invoice or write "cancel" on the invoice and owe nothing. The initial response to this type of offer can be one to three percent. However, the final membership payment rate can be as high as 50 percent.

- **Negative Option Free Trial**
  Under this method, when a free trial is accepted the respondent provides credit card information and has a limited period of time to evaluate the membership. If the trial is cancelled by the respondent, there is no charge. However, if no notice is given, then the credit card is charged for the membership. Conversion rates for this approach were not measured in the case studies I examined.

In any case, the trial membership model is ideal if, and only if, the product or service offered during the trial is one prospective members' are likely to build reliance on. The **American College of Surgeons** (ACS) provides a 30-day trial consisting of access to the association's members-only web portal. The trial advertises that prospects will have access to a variety of features typically available only to ACS members. I'm not convinced this is a strong offer, but I'm not a surgeon and I'm not sure what is available on the members-only portion of the ACS site. Perhaps it is a hot commodity that surgeons are seeking.

Trial membership may or may not be a viable option for your association. The ticket is to respond to what your membership wants and what makes the most sense for your association's unique needs.

The **Society of Nonprofit Organizations** (SNPO) replaced its 30-day trial membership offer with a free associate membership program. While the trial membership was limited to 30 days and included only a month's worth of publications, the associate membership provides ongoing access to the entire archive of

SNPO publications as well as access to job postings and grant information.

The models listed here are merely examples of ways in which your association could reinvent itself. What works for one association doesn't always work for another. There isn't a quick-fix solution, and there certainly isn't going to be a return to the "one-size-fits-all" membership model either.

Every association has to analyze how recent changes in the economy, demographics, and technology have affected their operations and their members. Some associations will find that their members want to pay dues to receive certain benefits. Others will be more successful with an a la carte model, and still others will be successful without dues. Businesses write business plans, and your association should write a new plan for engaging members and increasing value through improved operations. Do the research. Listen to your members. Get creative. Try new strategies. Whatever you do, do something.

Bottom line: It doesn't really matter how you sell. What sells is what the buyer wants.

7

Building a Next Century Association

"Fortune befriends the bold."
Emily Dickinson

An association executive slips and falls off the edge of a cliff. On the way down, he manages to grab onto the end of a vine. He's hanging there, a thousand feet from the top and a thousand feet from the bottom. His situation seems hopeless, so he looks up to the clouds and begins to pray. "Is anybody up there?" he asks. After a long silence, a deep voice bellows down from the clouds: *"Do you believe?"* "Yes," replies the association executive. *"Then let go of the vine,"* says the voice. The association executive pauses for a moment, looks up again, and finally responds, "Is there anybody else up there?"

I've heard that joke made in reference to entrepreneurs and it's equally fitting for association executives. Actually, it's fitting for anyone in a leadership role, because most leaders are simply not ready to let go of the vine.

You might know the feeling; You want membership to grow, but at the same time you're frustrated, tired, and unwilling to take any more risk. Your association once stood alone as a prominent leader, prosperous, plentiful, and unscathed by competition. Now your association's foundation is crumbling, beaten down by the winds of change: economic decline, demographic shifts and rapidly changing technology.

If you're not happy with the current state of your association, you have three choices. You can live with it, close it, or change it. If the first two choices aren't an option, it's time to make changes. It's time to let go of the vine.

A Safety Net

Change can be scary, but with the right vision and structure in place, your association can evolve and realize its full potential again. This book was designed to equip you with the information and ideas needed to rebuild your association. In this final chapter, you'll find an actual plan so your association can successfully make the move from building to boomtown. Consider this your safety net. If your association takes the time to heed this advice and plan for its future success, you'll be able to let go of the vine and land on higher ground.

The following steps are an organized compilation of the advice shared in the previous six chapters. Don't underestimate the value of this chapter. All the secrets are here. Associations have paid me handsomely to develop customized strategic plans for their membership growth. This chapter breaks the process down so your association can achieve the same results without the aid of outside help.

The goal is to help you optimize your association's value, thereby eliminating the competition and giving members a reason to join. Equally important is that your association reduces the burden of unnecessary costs or operations that don't add enough value or simply make it difficult for your audience to engage. The process takes time and effort, but in the end, the effort will be worth it because your association will observe increases in membership and revenues. Here's exactly what your association needs to do to flip its fortune.

Step 1: Focus

In a previous chapter I mentioned an association that had 10 target markets. Not surprising, the programming of this association was all over the board, as was everything from internal operations to chapter and committee management. The staff was unwieldy and inefficient, every decision—from which industry should be represented on the board to which books should be carried in the store—was challenging, and members were always complaining.

I met with the staff and the board and interviewed several members. No one (and I mean no one) in that association was happy. Everyone was frustrated, confused, or felt slighted because the association lacked focus. The association kept getting distracted by new opportunities and audiences and, as a result, became diluted and lost value.

First and foremost, your association leadership should define, with absolute clarity, your association's reason for being and its niche. Why does your association exist? What makes your association unique? Chances are you already have a focus but you need to make sure your association isn't distracted. Identify where your association needs to be to best serve its purpose, then cut out any unnecessary effort, expense, or programming that distracts from that purpose.

Step 2: Goal-Setting

Every successful enterprise is successful because it sets goals and works diligently to achieve those goals. When the economy flattened, most organizations lost sight of their goals and just did what they needed to do to survive. It's time to get back to the future. If you're focusing on day-to-day operations, you won't make much progress and you certainly aren't going to reach any BHAGs (big, hairy, audacious goals).

It's easy to set short-term goals, but I want you to set a stretch goal—something with significance. Meet with your leadership team and discuss where you want to take your association. Ask them to think about where they want the association to be five years from now. Some associations prefer to set goals out even farther—maybe 10 years out. There's no right or wrong, just take into consideration how much change has happened in the past three years to alter your association's very existence. To me, it makes more sense to focus on a five-year goal.

It may take time to reach a consensus, so make sure you allow time to find a goal that motivates everyone. You want your team to be really inspired and excited about meeting this goal. Mediocre goals are simply not worth the effort.

Step 3: Marketing

If you want to sell more memberships, you've got to know exactly who would benefit from having a membership in your association. As with the first point—focus—it's far superior for your association to be of value to a few people than to try to be everything to everyone. Marketing success relies on a four-step process.

First, determine what differentiates your association from its competition. For this step, you may want to survey or interview members and also request the feedback of your membership sales team. Ask what members really like about your association. Why do they choose to join your association and not some other association? Compile the list of answers then determine which three aspects of your association your members value most. You've not only determined what makes you unique; you've determined what makes a membership in your association valuable. This is really important information.

Next, determine your guarantee. As an association executive, you may be familiar with Ron Rosenberg. He's a consultant on the topic of "business self-defense" and speaks often at association events. Ron always encourages his audience to have a guarantee. He even suggests that associations should offer money back to any member who is dissatisfied. Ron will tell you that if you can't guarantee your programming or membership, then you're probably delivering a sub-par product. A guarantee is the opportunity to put members' minds at ease and enables you to sell more memberships, programs, products, or services. Meet with your leadership team and list what you believe to be the biggest frustrations, fears, and worries of your potential customers. List all the possible guarantees you'd be willing to offer to put their minds at ease.

The third step is to identify your core benefits. In business, it's referred to as a proven process; a step-by-step for how businesses work with their clients to ensure greater success. As a membership association, you need to highlight your deliverables—what you give to members to solve their problems and bring them more success. Examine how you position these benefits. Focus on outcomes, not features, and measurable success whenever possible. Refer to Chapter 3 for more guidance on this topic.

The final step is to determine your target market. These are your ideal members, the ones most likely to purchase, benefit from, and really value a membership in your association. In Chapter 4, I argued that your association should tailor more of its efforts to younger prospects. These members hold the greatest potential for growth and they are, to put it candidly, the only possible succession plan for your association.

In addition, the more you know about your target market, the better your chances of success. Take a look at your existing membership. Who is most engaged and why? What problems does your association solve for them? Put thought into your target membership and develop a list based on their key characteristics: geography, industry, title, age range, and other pertinent factors. Create a list of prospects compiled from current prospect lists, referrals from current members, trade publications, purchasing lists, and member lists of like-minded groups on LinkedIn.

Remember, the best way to reach prospects is through relationships. Even if you have a list of perfect prospects, if you're approaching them armed with sales pitches, expect your efforts to fall flat. When you have a great offer that isn't based on fluff and meaningless chatter, then you have a precise, proven, and meaningful strategy for rebuilding your membership dominance.

Step 4: Troubleshooting

Identify your association's obstacles to growth and potential solutions for overcoming those obstacles. Most of the obstacles associations are facing are addressed in this book: declining value, outdated member benefits, outdated technology, aging membership, and declining revenues. Perhaps you need to revamp your dues structure, introduce new technology or membership models, or target younger audiences. Whatever the case may be, eliminate the negative influences and focus on your association's potential. After you've identified where you want to take your association in the future, identifying and removing obstacles is especially imperative to ensuring your success.

Ask your leadership team to think of the obstacles, concerns, and opportunities you face in achieving your goals. List all the challenges; then whittle down the list to the top three challenges that need to be addressed. Discuss the real problems behind your list of three challenges. You have aging membership or declining revenues for a reason. Try to pinpoint what those reasons are.

Next, discuss possible solutions for resolving those challenges. This means identifying action items and people responsible for implementing those action items to effectively eliminate the challenge. Troubleshooting is perhaps the most difficult step, and it takes time and energy because no one really enjoys trouble-shooting, airing out issues, or discussing change. You may want to hire an outside facilitator for troubleshooting. It is a critical step, so don't skip it. Just be aware that it can be challenging to overcome your challenges. Your team may want to identify the challenges first, and then come back to the solutions discussion after step 5 is complete.

Step 5: Targeted Progress

Now it's time to take all this strategy and implement it into day-to-day operations. This means making decisions about what you must get done this year, and tracking your progress to ensure unparalleled success. Schedule a meeting with your leadership team and determine the retention, recruiting, revenue, and profit goals your team would like to achieve within the next year.

Next, decide on three to seven priorities that must be completed this year for you to be on track with your five-year goals. These one-year goals need to be measurable, attainable, and specific. An outsider should be able to read your goals and know exactly what you mean and how you will measure success. Don't just write down that you want to increase retention. Write down that you want to increase retention from 85 percent to 92 percent.

Make sure you have a projected budget to support your plan. This will confirm that you have all of the resources you need to achieve the plan and that when you achieve the revenue goal, the profit number is realistic. Then break the year into quarters; 90 days of work toward reaching your goals. These 90-day targets are the most efficient, profitable means for planning your work and working your plan.

The greatest failure is not in failing to plan but in failing to implement a plan. Association executives will invest time and resources into the plan development, but somewhere along the line they forget that they must actually implement the plan if it is to work. Holding the finished plan in your hands will do nothing to help your association. You must act on it, and the 90-day targets are there to help ease the load, make it more manageable, help you track your progress, and experience success every step of the way. It's designed to make the implementation process as expedient and rewarding as possible, so don't stop at this step.

The following chart will help you stay focused on your plan. Copy it and hang it everywhere in your association's office. Make sure it's visible so it's always top of mind and everyone knows exactly where you are headed as an organization.

Letting Go

If you're looking for a cheat sheet for building a membership dominance, the advice in this book comes down to six key points:

1. Understand what your members want and need.

2. Develop member benefits that solve the problems of your target audience.

3. Assess the costs to provide those benefits and get rid of anything that doesn't provide a benefit.

4. Put a membership model in place that both aligns with the way your audience wants to pay to have their problems solved and makes it easy for your offering to sell.

Membership Building Plan

Focus	5-Year Vision
Purpose/Passion: Niche:	Date: Retention: Recruiting Revenue: Profit: Our vision:

Marketing Strategy	Challenges & Solutions
Member Values: 1. 2. 3. Guarantee to Members: Core Member Benefits: 1. 2. 3. Target Membership Market:	Challenges: 1. 2. 3. Solutions: 1. 2. 3.

One Year Goal	90-Day Targets
Date: Retention: Recruiting Revenue: Profit: Goals: 1. 2. 3.	Quarter 1 Date: Retention: Recruiting Revenue: Profit: Quarter Goals: 1. 2. 3.

5. Test these offerings and revenue models with members and nonmembers. Make adjustments accordingly.

6. Repeat.

If you're looking for one piece of light-a-fire information it's this: Change or die. There are no alternatives.

And if you want reassurance that everything will be all right, you have it right here in the palm of your hands. If you follow the advice in this book, you have a chance to alter your association's destiny. This is your opportunity to flip your fortune and build a membership-attracting, revenue-generating organization. So what are you waiting for?

Let go of the vine.

Index